Jesus and Paul

Places They Knew

by

F. F. Bruce

Thomas Nelson Publishers
Nashville • Camden • New York

Contents

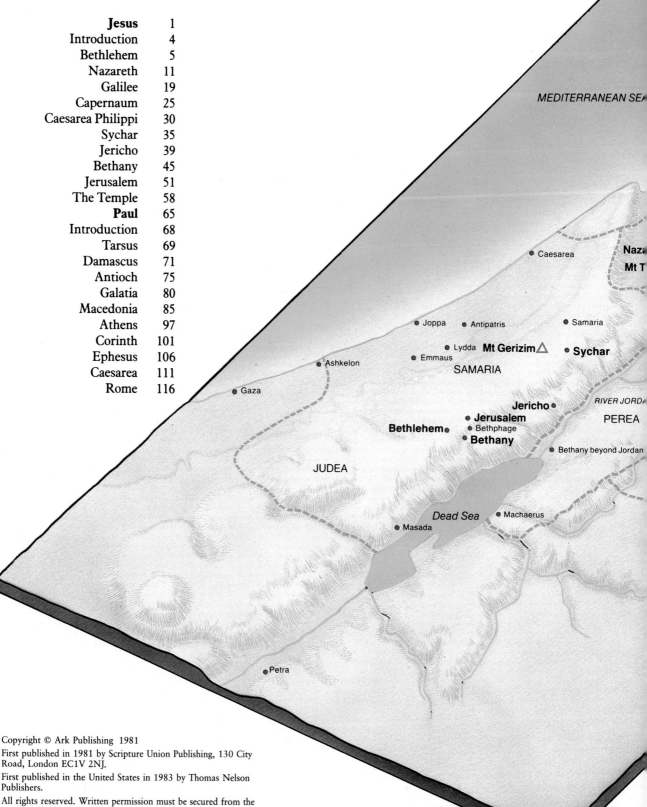

MEDITERRANEAN SEA

Caesarea

Naza
Mt T

Joppa Antipatris Samaria

Lydda Mt Gerizim △ **Sychar**
Emmaus

Ashkelon SAMARIA

Gaza

Jericho RIVER JORDA

Jerusalem PEREA

Bethlehem Bethphage
Bethany

Bethany beyond Jordan

JUDEA

Dead Sea Machaerus

Masada

Petra

First published in 1981 by Scripture Union Publishing, 130 City Road, London EC1V 2NJ.

First published in the United States in 1983 by Thomas Nelson Publishers.

Published in Nashville, Tennessee, by Thomas Nelson, Inc. and distributed in Canada by Lawson Falle, Ltd., Cambridge, Ontario.
ISBN 0-8407-5281-4

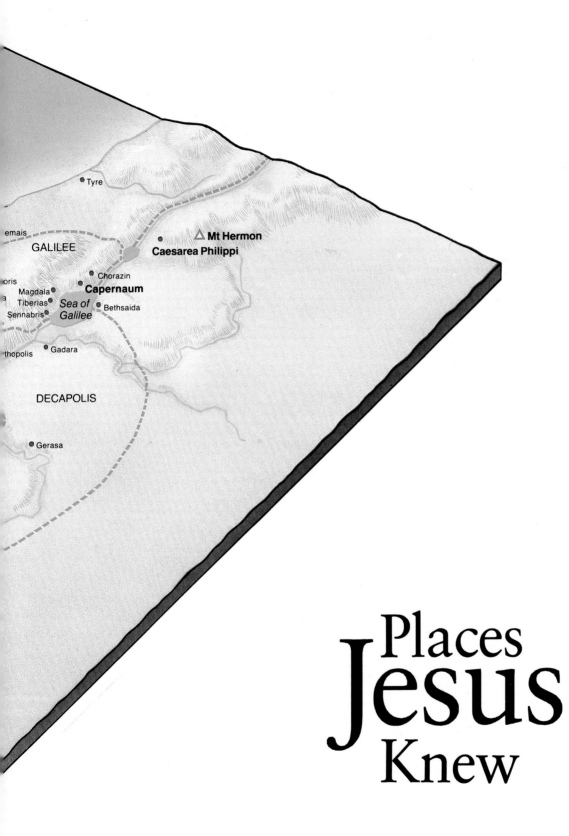

Tyre

emais

GALILEE

△ **Mt Hermon**

Caesarea Philippi

oris

Chorazin

Magdala

Capernaum

Tiberias

Sea of Galilee

Bethsaida

Sennabris

thopolis

Gadara

DECAPOLIS

Gerasa

Places
Jesus
Knew

Introduction

The people and events described in the Bible were very much down-to-earth; they did not belong to some never-never land above the clouds. Some of the men and women whom we meet in the Bible lived all their lives in the same place; many others travelled widely. While Jesus taught for three years only, mainly within Palestine, Paul's extensive journeys took him through the Roman Empire around the Mediterranean Sea. If we can envisage them in their various geographical settings, it helps us to understand many of the things that are recorded about them.

Many features of the Bible lands have changed between those earlier days and our own. The Bedouin tents may still look much as they did in Abraham's time, but the people who live in them today keep in touch with domestic and international news with the aid of transistor radios, which gives them a different outlook on the world. But we can still appreciate the difference between the desert where they live and the cultivated land which adjoins it, or the difference between country life and city life. Egypt's fertility still depends on the Nile, and Syria and the Holy Land still depend on seasonal rainfall for regular harvests.

Human life was controlled by natural conditions in Bible days, and to a large extent it still is. To learn something, therefore, of the places which the Bible characters knew is a great help to seeing their lives and actions in a proper context. The best way to learn, no doubt, is to visit the places ourselves and picture the persons and events associated with them. But if that cannot be done, then photographs and verbal descriptions will do something to fill the gap. Some of the places are still busy centres of human activity; others have been excavated after being covered over for centuries and stand as relics of what once was. Either way, they can teach us something about the Bible story.

F. F. BRUCE

Bethlehem

Bethlehem is first mentioned in the Bible in the story of Jacob's return to his homeland from Mesopotamia. According to Genesis 35:19 Rachel died and was buried 'on the way to Ephrath (that is, Bethlehem)', where her tomb is still shown. This explains 'Rachel weeping for her children' after Herod's massacre of the infants of Bethlehem (Matthew 2:16-18).

The name of the town originally meant 'house of Lahmu' (who was evidently a Canaanite divinity); to the Jews it came to mean 'house of bread'. After the Israelite settlement in Canaan it was allocated to the tribe of Judah. It was the home of the Levite who appears in the story of Micah (Judges 17:7); it was also the home of the ill-fated concubine of another Levite (Judges 19:1). It plays a happier part in the story of Ruth, as the home of Elimelech and Naomi and then as the home of Boaz and Ruth. The book of Ruth ends with a family tree showing how King David was the great-grandson of Boaz and Ruth. It was the fact that David was born and brought up there that gave Bethlehem its fame in Old Testament times. Otherwise it was an unimportant place, not figuring significantly in the history of the monarchy; but in the days when the fortunes of the kingdom of Judah were at a low ebb, the prophet Micah foretold that a ruler would arise from Bethlehem and restore his people's fortunes.

This oracle from Micah 5:2 is quoted in Matthew's nativity narrative, in his account of the visit of the Magi. When they arrived in Jerusalem, asking for the whereabouts of the new-born king of the Jews, they were directed to Herod's palace. Herod summoned the leading rabbis and asked them where the Messiah was to be born. 'In Bethlehem of Judea,' they said, for this was the place indicated by the prophet (Matthew 2:3-6).

Luke, in his nativity narrative, brings Joseph and Mary to Bethlehem immedi-

The traditional site of Jesus' birth in a cave below the Church of the Nativity is marked with a star.

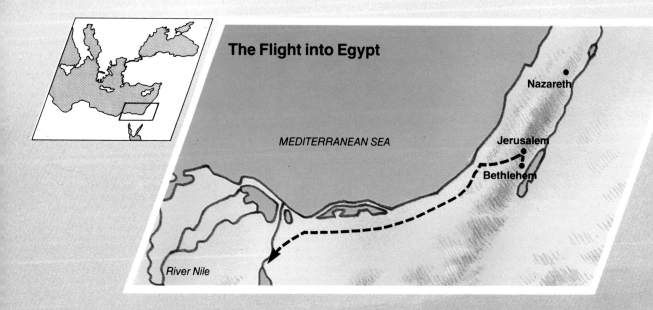

The Flight into Egypt

MEDITERRANEAN SEA

Nazareth

Jerusalem

Bethlehem

River Nile

A shepherd and his flock in the hills of Judea near Bethlehem.

ately before the birth of Jesus because the Roman Emperor, Augustus, had decreed an empire-wide census. The census regulations required that everyone should return to his family home to be enrolled – especially, one supposes, if he or his family owned property there. Joseph, being a member of the family of David, returned to Bethlehem and took his newly-wedded wife with him. There is an impressive contrast, no doubt designed, between the most powerful ruler in the world, issuing his edict from the Palatine in Rome and the child whose birthplace was, as an incidental consequence of that edict, in an obscure corner of the empire – a child who was destined nevertheless to wield more extended sovereignty than Augustus ever commanded (Luke 2:1-7).

Houses in the rocky hills of Judea.

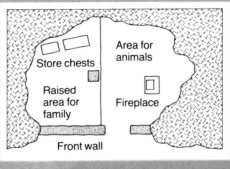

Store chests

Area for animals

Raised area for family

Fireplace

Front wall

An artist's impression of a typical cave dwelling.

8 **Bethlehem**

The bell-tower of the Church of the Nativity.

Looking north across the Judean hills to Jerusalem. The golden Dome of the Rock marks the site of the Temple where Jesus was dedicated.

Matthew and Luke are quite independent of each other in their nativity narratives, but they agree that Jesus was born in Bethlehem, that his mother was a virgin when she conceived him, and that Joseph, her husband and Jesus' legal father, was a descendant of David.

In the middle of the second century AD Justin Martyr reports that, since Joseph found nowhere to lodge in Bethlehem itself, he put up in a 'cave' near the village. Justin, as a native of Palestine, may well have known a local tradition that the birthplace of Jesus was a cave used as a stable. Origen of Alexandria, who spent the last twenty-three years of his life (from AD 231 onwards) at Caesarea in Palestine, knew the same tradition. 'At Bethlehem,' he says, 'there is shown the cave where Jesus was born, and the manger in which he lay wrapped in swaddling bands. Indeed, this sight is much mentioned in the places around, even among enemies of the faith: "In this place," they say, "Jesus was born, he who is worshipped and reverenced by the Christians."'

Even today, in the neighbourhood of Bethlehem, one may occasionally find a cave here and there used (if conveniently close to the owner's house) as a stable, with a manger attached to the wall. It is conceivable, indeed, that such a house might be built near a cave for precisely that reason.

It was probably in recognition of the local tradition, known to Justin and Origen, that the Emperor Constantine built over the cave the basilica which was the first Church of the Nativity; it was dedicated in AD 339, two years after Constantine's death. The present Church of the Nativity, on the same site, is basically the work of the Emperor Justinian (AD 527-565). In the course of excavations carried out in 1934 the mosaic floor of Constantine's basilica was brought to light, together with the foundations of its walls.

The angel's announcement to the shepherds of the Saviour's birth (Luke 2:8-18) was early commemorated by a Byzantine church in the area east of the town, called the Shepherds' Fields. In the crypt beneath its ruins Orthodox services are still held.

After his family left Bethlehem there is no record of Jesus' ever visiting the place again. His early association with it was not generally known. Hence, when some of his hearers on one occasion in Jerusalem thought he must be the Messiah, others said that this was impossible, for this man (as everyone knew) was a Galilean, whereas 'the Messiah is descended from David, and

Bethlehem from fields to the east, in the area where angels announced Jesus' birth to the shepherds.

comes from Bethlehem, the village where David was' (John 7:42). John implies that he and his readers share the knowledge of Jesus' actual birthplace, of which most of Jesus' contemporaries were ignorant; this is an instance of what is called 'Johannine irony'.

Bethlehem today is an Arab city, the seat of an Arab university. A large proportion of its Arab population is Christian.

Biblical references Matthew 2:6
Here Micah 5:2 is quoted, but with a difference. The oracle in Micah begins: 'But you, O Bethlehem Ephrathah, who are little to be among the clans of Judah . . .' The place once described as 'little' has now become 'not the least', which means in effect 'very great'. It is the birth of Christ there that justifies the change. Note also: Micah continues the oracle beyond the point where Matthew breaks off the quotation: he goes on to say, 'whose origin is from of old, from ancient days'. We might consider how these last words could be true of the child who was born in Bethlehem.

Bethlehem at dusk; David's city was the birthplace of Christianity.

Nazareth

Nazareth was a small town in Galilee, about fifteen miles west of the Lake of Galilee and twenty miles east of the Mediterranean, where Joseph and Mary lived and where Jesus was brought up from early childhood. Jesus was therefore commonly known as 'Jesus of Nazareth' or 'Jesus the Nazarene'; and it was probably because of their association with him that his followers, in turn, came to be called Nazarenes.

Nazareth does not appear to have been a place of any significance in antiquity. It is nowhere mentioned in the Old Testament or in pre-Christian Jewish literature. The first reference to it outside Christian literature is in a fragmentary inscription found in the ancient synagogue of Caesarea in 1962, where it is named as one of the places in Galilee where the members of the twenty-four priestly divisions settled after the crushing of the second Jewish revolt against Rome in AD 135. The particular division

The hills and fertile land of Galilee, where Jesus grew up and began his ministry.

Looking south over Nazareth towards the Plain of Esdraelon. The Church of the Annunciation commemorates the angel's visit to Mary.

St Mary's Well, where Jesus' family would have drawn fresh water.

that settled in Nazareth was that of Happizzez (1 Chronicles 24:15).

Nathanael's question, 'Can anything good come out of Nazareth?' (John 1:46), suggests that it enjoyed no great reputation among its neighbours. In the narrative of Jesus' public ministry Nazareth does not appear in a very favourable light. Mark and Matthew relate that, when Jesus visited the place soon after the beginning of his Galilean ministry, his fellow-townsmen gave him no credence and therefore did not witness any of his mighty works, apart from the healing of a few sick people (Mark 6:1-6; Matthew 13:53-58). Luke adds a summary of his sabbath-day address in the synagogue, where he took as his text the opening words of Isaiah 61. Jesus explained that his present ministry was to proclaim 'the acceptable year of the Lord', implying that he himself was the Spirit-anointed speaker of the passage which he read. The address aroused so much hostility among

his hearers that they tried to throw him over 'the brow of the hill on which their city was built' (Luke 4:29) – which is still pointed out as the Mount of Precipitation.

There is an inscribed marble slab in the Louvre in Paris known as the 'Nazareth inscription' because it was sent to France from Nazareth by the collector W. Froehner in 1878. It cannot be established that it was actually set up in Nazareth. It contains the text of a Roman imperial edict, commonly ascribed to Claudius (AD 41-54), forbidding the disturbance of tombs. Whether or not this edict (which in any case only restated existing legislation) was a reaction to reports of the empty tomb of Jesus, there is no means of knowing for certain.

Nazareth was a small Jewish village in the early fourth century AD, according to Eusebius of Caesarea. The earliest recorded church in the town is mentioned by a seventh-century writer; it had formerly been a synagogue. Excavations have revealed traces of an earlier church, dating from the beginning of the fifth century. A magnificent basilica was built there in the twelfth century, during the Crusader domination of Palestine, when Nazareth was the seat of an archbishop. After the

The people of Nazareth tried to throw Jesus from the hilltop, now known as the 'Mount of Precipitation', after his teaching in the synagogue.

Mount Tabor and the Plain of Esdraelon seen from Mount Carmel. Nazareth lies among the hills in the distance to the left.

expulsion of the Crusaders, Nazareth was destroyed by order of Sultan Baybars in 1263. It lay derelict for 400 years. Its rehabilitation as a Christian shrine dates from the seventeenth century, when the Franciscans were recognised as guardians of the holy places.

Nazareth is now a city of over 20,000 population, inhabited mainly by Arab Christians. It is indeed the largest Christian city in Israel. The great new Church of the Annunciation, commemorating the incident of Luke 1:26-38, was begun in 1955; the excavating of its foundations provided an opportunity to explore the remains of the Byzantine church which stood on the same site, but also brought evidence to light that the place had been occupied as early as the Middle Bronze Age (around the seventeenth century BC). There can be no certainty that the church actually stands on the site of Mary's house, any more than that St. Joseph's Church stands on the site of Joseph's workshop. The one place in Nazareth which can with confidence be associated with Jesus' family is St. Mary's Well, from which water has been drawn from time immemorial.

Here then in Nazareth Jesus grew up, with four younger brothers and an unknown number of sisters. It is precarious to try to fill in the details of those 'hidden years'. But from the high ground above the town a boy like Jesus, interested in the Old Testament writings, could look down on many scenes which figured in the earlier history of his people. To the south stretched the plain of Esdraelon (the valley of Jezreel), which had witnessed a succession of great battles, including Barak's victory over Sisera and good King Josiah's fatal defeat at Megiddo. Beyond the plain of Esdraelon, slightly to the left, was Mount Gilboa, where King Saul had fallen in battle against the Philistines. To the east rose Mount Tabor, 1843 feet high, later to be the traditional (but doubtful) site of the Transfiguration. South-west of Tabor lies the small town of Nain, where Jesus was to restore a widow's son to life as he was being carried out of the town to be buried (Luke 7:11-17). Two or three miles beyond Nain was Shunem, where Elisha's generous hostess had lived (2 Kings 4:8). About nine miles north-east of Nazareth was Cana (if it is to be identified with the modern Khirbet Qana), the home of Nathanael (John 21:2), where Jesus was to perform his 'beginning of miracles' by turning water into wine (John 2:1-11).

Nazareth lay off the beaten track, but the road from the lake of Galilee to Ptolemais (Acco) ran a few miles to the north, while the great 'Way of the Sea' from Damascus and farther north passed by not far to the south, leading to the Mediterranean coast and so south to Egypt. Along it, in both directions, moved trading caravans and

Moonrise over Nain, a village where Jesus brought a widow's son back to life.

Wild flowers cover the Galilean hills in the spring.

detachments of soldiers. Galilee at that time was part of the tetrarchy of Herod Antipas, youngest son of the late Herod the Great, and not a Roman province (as Judea was); so any Roman soldiers seen in Galilee would be seconded to his service. But Herod Antipas ruled by grace of the Romans, and the Roman presence was never far from people's thoughts, even in Galilee. When Jesus was about nine years old, everyone was talking about the rebellion in Judea led by Judas, a Galilean from Gamala, east of the lake. (In popular usage the term Galilee took in some territory east of the lake as well as the region to the west.) Judas and his followers raised the standard of revolt in AD 6 against

MEDITERRANEAN SEA

Chorazin

Capernaum

Magdala

Bethsaida

Tiberias

Sea of Galilee

Sepphoris

Cana

Nazareth

Mount Tabor

Gadara

Roman control of Judea and the obligation on its inhabitants to pay tribute to the emperor. The rising was crushed, and Judas perished (Acts 5:37), but his ideals lived on and found fresh champions from time to time.

The people of Nazareth, like the other Galileans, did not have to pay taxes to the emperor, but the issue which involved the Judeans must have been a matter of concern to many of them. Thoughtful boys in Nazareth must have discussed these matters and found their sympathies deeply engaged. What did Jesus think? We know what he thought in manhood when he answered the question put to him in the temple precincts in Jerusalem: 'Should we pay tribute to Caesar or not?' (Mark 12:17).

Biblical references John 1:46

'Can anything good come out of Nazareth?' asked Nathanael. If this was a popular saying in that part of Galilee, there may have been some ground for it. There are people who will allow such a piece of proverbial wisdom to prejudice them against entertaining the possibility that there could be an exception to the rule. Nathanael, happily, did not allow his mind to be prejudiced. He responded readily enough to Philip's invitation 'Come and see', and found that the greatest imaginable good came from such an unlikely place as Nazareth. A willingness to test the evidence for oneself is a sovereign remedy against prejudice.

The Sea of Galilee from the hills to the north-west. Fields of olive trees cover the slopes where Jesus travelled during his ministry in Galilee.

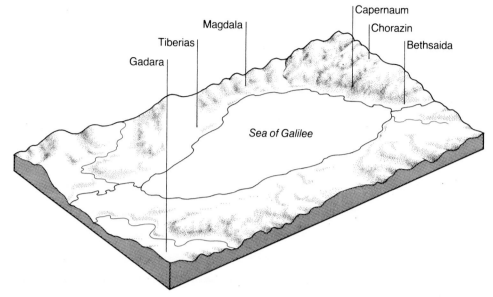

Gadara Tiberias Magdala Capernaum Chorazin Bethsaida

Sea of Galilee

The Sea of Galilee looking
north-west towards Magdala.

Galilee

The Lake (or Sea) of Galilee is a pear-shaped stretch of fresh water into which the Jordan flows from the north and out of which it flows towards the south. It is about thirteen miles long from north to south, and nearly eight miles across from west to east at its greatest width; it lies 695 feet below Mediterranean sea level and reaches a depth of about 200 feet.

Its Old Testament name is the Lake of Chinnereth: this word means 'lyre' and has been thought to refer to the shape of the lake, which can easily be seen in its entirety from the higher ground around it. If that is so, then the city of Chinnereth, mentioned in Deuteronomy 3:17 and elsewhere, must take its name from the lake; but if the lake takes its name from the city, the 'lyre-shape' explanation must be given up. In the New Testament it is called not only the Sea of Galilee but the Lake of Gennesaret (Luke 5:1), from the fertile plain on its north-west

Sunrise over the lake. Eucalyptus trees, planted recently in Israel, are not indigenous, but are part of a programme to replace trees cut down over the centuries for building.

side (modern Ginossar), and the Sea of Tiberias (John 6:1; 21:1), from the city which Herod Antipas built on its western shore about AD 22.

Much of Jesus' public ministry took place around the shores of the lake. One can still be impressed by the acoustic properties of some of the places from which he taught, whether from the slopes of the rising hill-country to the west (the Mount of the Beatitudes) or from a boat pushed a little way out to sea near Capernaum, from which the people on land could hear him as in a natural amphitheatre. Storms such as those described in the Gospel story still blow up suddenly, when currents of air from the west, passing through the Arbel valley, are sucked down in vortices over the lake.

In Jesus' time the territory west of the lake was ruled by Herod Antipas, tetrarch of Galilee from 4 BC to his deposition in AD 39. Herod's new capital of Tiberias (called after his patron, the Roman Emperor Tiberius) is not said to have been visited by Jesus. In fact, for a long time Jews tended to avoid it, regarding it as ceremonially unclean because it was built on the site of a cemetery. It may have been in his palace at Tiberias that Herod's macabre birthday party was held (Mark 6:21). If so, the messenger who carried the order for John the Baptist's execution had a long way to travel, for Josephus tells us that John was imprisoned and put to death in Herod's Transjordan fortress of Machaerus. Josephus is probably right: John was active in the lower Jordan valley, including 'Bethany beyond the Jordan' (John 1:28), which lay in Herod's territory of Perea. Before he built Tiberias, Herod lived in Sepphoris, four miles north-west of Nazareth. Rumours of goings-on at his court must have been current in Nazareth, and when some of Jesus' parables were set in royal courts his hearers would have a fair picture of the scene in their mind's eye.

Looking south across the Sea of Galilee down the Jordan Valley which leads to Jericho and the Dead Sea. Jesus taught crowds seated on the lower slopes from a boat pushed out from the shore.

East of the lake the ruler was Herod's brother, Philip the tetrarch (mentioned in Luke 3:1), whose capital was Caesarea Philippi (see p.30). Philip's territory was untroubled by the tension that made Herod Antipas so suspicious and cunning – it was not for nothing that Jesus called Antipas 'that fox' (Luke 13:32). When Antipas' interest in Jesus became too keen to be healthy, it was easy to avoid his attention by crossing to the other side of the lake.

The modern visitor finds it difficult to envisage the thriving towns which surrounded the lake in Jesus' day. The lake teemed with fish, which provided a living for many of the inhabitants of those towns. The fish they caught were not only sent to other parts of Palestine and Transjordan, but salted and exported to other lands. Magdala, between Capernaum and Tiberias, was given the Greek name of Tarichaeae, because of the salt fish (*tarichos* in Greek) which it exported. It was the home of Mary Magdalene. Capernaum, which Jesus chose as his headquarters during his ministry in Galilee (see p.19), is mentioned alongside Chorazin and Bethsaida in Matthew 11:20-24 and Luke 10:13-15. Doom is pronounced on all three because, although they had witnessed so many of Jesus' mighty works, they refused to repent.

Chorazin, two and a half miles north of Capernaum, was destroyed at the time of the second Jewish revolt against Rome (AD 132-135) but was rebuilt and remained a flourishing city for some generations, extending to an area of about twelve acres. By the time of Eusebius, however (about AD 330), it lay in ruins. It was well supplied with water. The buildings, including the synagogue, were of the local black basalt. The synagogue, many of whose walls still stand, occupied an area of about seventy by fifty feet. It was supported by pillars and pilasters whose capitals and cases repre-

sented a variety of Greek orders. It was richly decorated with floral designs enclosing human and animal figures, which suggest that its builders and sponsors did not take the second commandment too literally. One of the most interesting pieces of furniture in the synagogue, belonging to the third century AD, was 'Moses' seat' (compare Matthew 23:2), from which the law was read or expounded; it was an armchair of black basalt, decorated with a rosette on the back. Many Jewish houses of the same period have also been excavated, together with water reservoirs and a ritual bath.

Bethsaida, which simply means 'Fishertown', lay a little way east of the point where the Jordan enters the lake from the north. Philip the tetrarch enlarged it and changed its name to Julias, in honour of Julia, daughter of the Emperor Augustus. (This must have been not later than 2 BC, for in that year Julia fell into disgrace and was exiled.) It was the original home of Peter and Andrew, and also of Philip the apostle, according to John 1:44. In its neighbourhood the feeding of the five thousand most probably took place. (The traditional site of the feeding, at Tabgha, south-west of Capernaum, is difficult to accept.) Mark also records the healing of a blind man at Bethsaida (Mark 8:22-26).

If one continues round the lake in a clockwise direction, one comes to a place on the east shore called Kursi or Kersa, directly across from Magdala. It is fairly certainly here that the healing of the man possessed by the legion of demons took place. It is the one point on the east side of the lake where the steep hills come right down almost to the water's edge. The modern name preserves the ancient Gerasa or (better) Gergesa. There was a much more important Gerasa (modern Jerash) over forty miles to the south, on the main north-south road through Transjordan, but that had nothing to do with the place on the lakeside. If the region is called 'the country of the Gadarenes' (Matthew 8:28), that may be because the city of Gadara (modern Umm Qeis), nearly seven miles south-east of the lake and separated from it by the deep Yarmuk gorge, had property around here. The presence of a large herd of pigs in the vicinity is sufficient indication that the local people were Gentiles.

When the demon-possessed man was cured, 'he went away and began to pro-

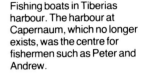

Fishing boats in Tiberias harbour. The harbour at Capernaum, which no longer exists, was the centre for fishermen such as Peter and Andrew.

The floor plan is all that remains of Chorazin's synagogue, once a richly decorated building with sculpted masonry. A human face from Chorazin.

claim in the Decapolis how much Jesus had done for him' (Mark 5:20). The Decapolis was a league of ten cities, the most northerly of which was Damascus and the most southerly Philadelphia (Amman); it included Gadara and Gerasa (Jerash). All but one of these cities – Scythopolis (Bethshean) – lay east of the Jordan valley. The term Decapolis may also denote, more generally, the area in which the ten cities lay – quite an extensive mission-field for the grateful man. Why did Jesus encourage him to spread the news of his recovery, whereas west of the lake he usually warned those whom he healed to keep quiet about it? Probably because the Decapolis was a Gentile area, where there was no danger of the revolutionary excitement that was always liable to break out among the Jews of Galilee.

Biblical references Matthew 4:18-20

It was by the 'Sea of Galilee' that Jesus called Simon Peter and Andrew from their fishing and promised to make them 'fishers of men'. It was by the same sea that, according to John 21:15-17, he appeared to his disciples in resurrection and recommissioned Peter to feed his sheep. The catching of fish may describe the work of an evangelist, but the feeding of sheep is the work of a pastor: both are essential. So, at the beginning of the ministry of the earthly Christ and at the beginning of the ministry of the risen Christ the Galilean lakeside provides an appropriate setting.

The Roman theatre at Scythopolis, modern Bethshean, which was the only town of the Decapolis west of the River Jordan.

Capernaum

Capernaum was the town on the western shore of the Lake of Galilee where Jesus made his headquarters when he came into Galilee preaching the good news of the kingdom of God after John the Baptist's imprisonment. Here Simon Peter and Andrew lived (Mark 1:29) although, according to John 1:44, they originally came from Bethsaida. Jesus preached in the synagogue of Capernaum one sabbath day early in his Galilean ministry and impressed the congregation by the authority with which he expelled a demon from a possessed man. On the same day, 'at even, when the sun did set', he cured a great number of sick people, so that his fame spread throughout the town and into the surrounding countryside (Mark 1:21-45).

It was in Capernaum, too, that he cured the paralysed man who was let down by his friends through a hole in the roof, and it was on the quayside of the town that he called Matthew-Levi to leave the collecting of taxes and follow him as a disciple (Mark 2:1-14). 'It was here, on the harbour steps at Capernaum,' wrote Dr. W.M. Christie, 'that Peter learned to swear. When he landed his fish, there sat Matthew, the publican, demanding his tax of one from every five ... And if ever cursing was justifiable, it was when such as Peter the fisherman cursed Matthew the publican.'

It was in Capernaum that the centurion lived whose servant was cured by an authoritative word from Jesus spoken at a distance. This centurion is said to have built the local synagogue as a token of his friendship for the Jewish community. He was presumably a non-commissioned officer from the Roman army seconded to the service of Herod Antipas. The relation of this healing narrative (Matthew 8:5-13; Luke 7:2-10) to that of the healing of the official's son in Capernaum by a word spoken in Cana (John 4:46-54) is debated; that official was also in Herod's service, but not necess-

Capernaum was the centre of Jesus' teaching in Galilee, and by one of his miracles he used two fishes and five loaves to feed a vast crowd on the slopes by the lake.

arily a member of his armed forces.

John tells us that it was in the Capernaum synagogue that Jesus delivered his discourse on the bread of life after the feeding of the five thousand (John 6:59).

But as time went on Jesus was no longer so welcome as a preacher in the synagogue as he was at the beginning of his ministry. In particular, his insistence on healing people there on the sabbath, even while the service was in progress, was felt by the synagogue authorities to be intolerable. So the mountain slope and the lakeside had to serve as his auditoria, but there he was heard by greater crowds than could be accommodated in the synagogue.

It was to Capernaum that Jesus and the disciples repeatedly returned from journeys throughout Galilee. Here, probably, he raised Jairus' daughter from her deathbed (Mark 5:21-43); here he taught his disciples the lesson of humility by the example of the child whom he set in their midst (Mark 9:33-37); here he discussed with Peter the propriety of paying the Temple tax and sent him to catch a fish to pay it for both of them (Matthew 17:24-27).

Capernaum, or Kefar Nahum, means 'the village of Nahum' – but it is not known which Nahum is meant. Josephus says that its hinterland was very fertile; he records how its inhabitants played an active part in the revolt against Rome which broke out in AD 66. It is mentioned also in rabbinical literature. But later its true location was forgotten for centuries. Well into the twentieth century two sites competed for identification with Capernaum, both on the north-west shore of the lake – Khirbet el-Minyeh, at the entrance to the Plain of Ginossar, and Tell Hum (as it is called by the Arabs), four miles to the north-east and three miles west of the place where the Jordan enters the lake. The Tell Hum identification has won the day, and rightly so: on Israeli road-signs and official maps Tell Hum is called Capernaum. The ruins of the town extend for a mile along the shore. The Arabic name Tell Hum does not imply (as place-names introduced by the element *tell* normally do) that there is a mound on the site covering layers of successive settlements. It is probably a corruption of Telonion, a name which was given to the place in the Middle Ages – and *telōnion* is simply the Greek word for 'tax office' in the story of Matthew-Levi's call to discipleship (Mark 2:14).

Excavations have been carried out on the site for many years, especially since 1894, when it was bought by the Franciscans and fenced round for security. The most imposing landmark on the site is the magnificently ornamented two-storey synagogue of white limestone, some sixty-five feet long, partly restored by the Franciscans. Its style of architecture and decoration, together with dedicatory inscriptions, suggest that it was built about the beginning of the third century AD. It was not the synagogue in which Jesus taught, though it may have been built on the site of that earlier one.

An octagonal church-building, with a fine mosaic floor, dates from the middle of

Capernaum was a town of some importance on the north-western shore of the lake. When Jesus gave the Sermon on the Mount above Capernaum, he may have referred to Safed on the skyline when he taught, 'You are the light of the world. A city on a hill cannot be hidden' (Matthew 5:14).

Part of the mosaic floor of a fifth-century church building in Capernaum. The town has been abandoned since the seventh century.

the fifteenth century. Its builders believed that it covered the site of Peter's house. This building replaced an earlier one on the site which was seen by the pilgrim Egeria in AD 383. 'In Capernaum,' she says, 'the house of the prince of the apostles has been made into a church, with its original walls still standing.' And excavations beneath the foundations of the octagonal church have uncovered the remains of a modest house, one room of which was apparently used as a chapel and bears signs of early Christian veneration.

The abandonment of the site of the town from the seventh century onwards may be thought to provide a commentary on Jesus' sad words: 'And you, Capernaum, will you be exalted to heaven? You shall be brought down to Hades. For if the mighty works done in you had been done in Sodom, it would have remained until this day' (Matthew 11:23; compare Luke 10:15).

The third-century synagogue, built of white limestone, may stand on the site where Jesus taught.

Biblical references Matthew 4:13

Leaving Nazareth, Jesus 'went and dwelt in Capernaum by the sea', and this is said to fulfil Isaiah's promise of blessing for 'Galilee of the Gentiles' (Isaiah 9:1). Not many Gentiles were directly blessed during Jesus' Galilean ministry: so far as Capernaum is concerned, the only exceptions recorded are the centurion and his servant (Matthew 8:5-13). But it was in Galilee, on an unnamed mountain, that the risen Christ appeared to the apostles and commissioned them to 'make disciples of all nations' (Matthew 28:19) – that is to say, Gentiles. Perhaps, then, Matthew reckoned that Isaiah's prophecy stretched forward into the world-wide mission which followed the resurrection of Christ.

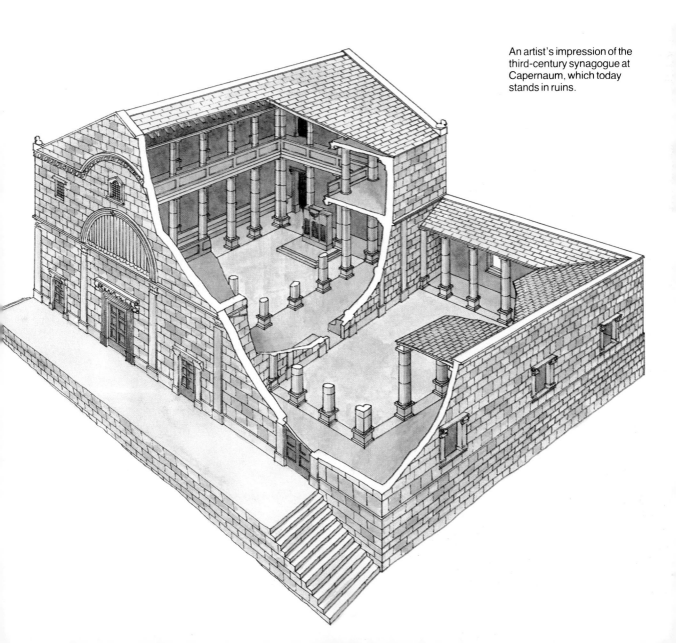

An artist's impression of the third-century synagogue at Capernaum, which today stands in ruins.

Caesarea Philippi

A flock of sheep at a waterhole in the hills. Jesus began to tell his disciples of his own death while in the district.

Caesarea Philippi figures only once in the gospel story. At the end of his Galilean ministry Jesus took his disciples away into the territory east and north of Galilee, and came with them 'to the villages of Caesarea Philippi' (Mark 8:27). He is not said to have visited the city of Caesarea Philippi itself: its 'villages' stood in the surrounding 'district' (Matthew 16:13), which it controlled. It was in this district that he asked his disciples who people said he was and then asked them what account they themselves had to give of him.

Caesarea Philippi is the modern Banyas, standing on a terrace about 1,150 feet high, at the foot of Mount Hermon. Mount Hermon rises on the north-east to a height of 9,100 feet. The Nahr Banyas, one of the principal sources of the Jordan, springs from a cave in the cliff-face here, and waters the whole terrace.

Poppy fields below Mount Hermon in the Golan Heights north-east of Galilee. Caesarea Philippi lay at the foot of Mount Hermon and was the centre of Philip's tetrarchy.

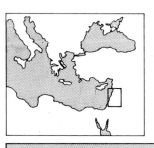

The spot was probably frequented as a shrine in antiquity. It is widely thought to have been the place mentioned in Joshua 11:17 as the northernmost limit of Joshua's conquest: 'Baal-gad in the valley of Lebanon below Mount Hermon.' Baal-gad means 'lord of fortune' and was presumably the divinity worshipped at the place called by his name. But this is speculation – we are on firmer footing when we come to the Greek period.

Shortly after the conquest of this area by Alexander the Great (332 BC), the Greeks dedicated the grotto from which Nahr Banyas springs 'to Pan and the Nymphs' (as we know from an inscription on the rock-face). From its dedication to Pan the shrine was called the Paneion and the city and district were called Paneias. Here, in 200 BC, a decisive battle was fought between the Seleucid king of Syria and the Ptolemaic king of Egypt. As a result of this battle, which the Seleucid king won,

Lebanon and Palestine became part of his kingdom and were henceforth ruled from Antioch, instead of being ruled from Alexandria, the capital of the Ptolemaic kingdom, as they had been for over a century. This battle, between 'the king of the north' (Antiochus III) and 'the king of the south' (Ptolemy V), is mentioned in Daniel 11:15,16, where the 'well-fortified city' is Paneias and 'the glorious land' is Palestine – or perhaps, more strictly, Judea.

In 64 and 63 BC the district of Paneias, with the whole of Syria and Palestine, came under the control of Rome. In due course Paneias was added by the Emperor Augustus to the kingdom of Herod the Great, who acknowledged the gift by erecting a marble temple in honour of Augustus. When Herod died in 4 BC, Paneias was included in the territory east and north of the lake of Galilee bequeathed to his son Philip the tetrarch (mentioned in Luke 3:1). Philip refounded Paneias as the capital of his tet-

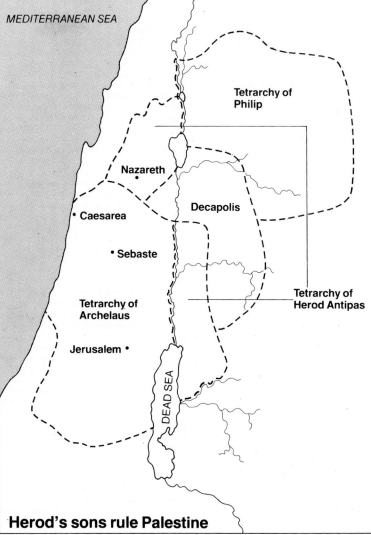

Herod's sons rule Palestine

rarchy and, by way of compliment to Augustus, who had confirmed Herod's bequest, renamed the city Caesarea. To distinguish it from Caesarea on the Mediterranean seaboard of Palestine (founded by Herod several years before and named in honour of the same emperor), this was commonly known as 'Philip's Caesarea' – in Latin, Caesarea Philippi. Philip was the most moderate of all Herod's sons who succeeded to parts of his kingdom – partly, no doubt, because his subjects were mainly Gentiles. When tension mounted in Galilee, and it became expedient for Jesus and his disciples to avoid the attention of Herod Antipas, it was easy for them to get into a boat and cross the lake into Philip's territory.

Twenty years after Philip's death (in AD 34), his grand-nephew the younger Agrippa (whom Paul could not altogether persuade to be a Christian) received Caesarea Philippi as the capital of his kingdom (which covered more or less the former tet-rarchy of Philip). He gave it the new name Neronias, as a compliment, this time, to the Emperor Nero. This new name did not last very long. Later, with the recession of Greek and Roman influence in those parts, and the reassertion of Semitic dominance, the name Caesarea Philippi also fell into disuse. The name which survived was Paneias, originally a Greek name, but altered in time to Banyas because of the Arabs' difficulty in pronouncing the 'p' sound.

Not much of the ancient architecture of Caesarea Philippi remains intact: hewn stones are scattered all over the site.

Josephus relates a story intended to prove that the spring of Banyas was fed by an underground stream from the circular Lake Phiale (the modern Birket Ram), seven miles to the east. But there is no connection between them: Lake Phiale is the water-filled crater of an extinct volcano.

The events in the district of Caesarea Philippi marked the end of one phase in

The upper reaches of the River Jordan, which flows from Caesarea Philippi into the Sea of Galilee. After Galilee, the river water is tapped heavily for irrigation, and the sluggish flow ends in the Dead Sea.

The Greeks dedicated shrines to Pan over one of the sources of the Jordan in a cave at Banyas.

Jesus' ministry and the beginning of a new one. When, in response to his question, 'But who do you say that I am?' (Mark 8:29), Peter confessed him to be the Messiah, he began to tell his disciples, to their shocked bewilderment, that this involved his suffering and death. His Galilean ministry had now come to an end, and soon afterwards, for the last time, he set out with them on the southward road to Judea and Jerusalem.

The Herods

	Herod the Great King of Judea			
	Archelaus	Herod Antipas	Philip	4 BC / AD
	Roman Procurator			6
	JUDEA	GALILEE	ITUREA AND TRACHONITIS	
			Roman Procurator	34
		Herod Agrippa I	Herod Agrippa I	37
Herod Agrippa I	Herod Agrippa I			
Roman Procurator	Roman Procurator	Roman Procurator		44
Felix		Herod Agrippa II		48 / 52- / 59 (?)
			70	

Biblical references Mark 8:27-30

Jesus' question, 'Who do men say that I am?' receives an even greater variety of answers today than it did when it was first put to the disciples in the neighbourhood of Caesarea Philippi. One interesting point about this question (and still more so about the personal question which followed, 'But who do *you* say that I am?') is that the answer tells us much more about the person who gives it than it tells us about Jesus. 'Indeed, it may be said of all theological schools of thought: "By their Lives of Jesus ye shall know them"' (T. W. Manson).

Sychar

Sychar, near which Jesus held his conversation with the woman at the well, is described in John 4:5 as 'a city of Samaria . . . near the field that Jacob gave to his son Joseph'. The field, or piece of land, which Jacob gave to Joseph is mentioned in Genesis 48:22, where Jacob on his deathbed says to Joseph, 'I have given to you rather than to your brothers one mountain slope (Hebrew *shechem*, 'shoulder') which I took from the hand of the Amorites with my sword and with my bow'. This military exploit is otherwise unchronicled in the Old Testament: it is hardly to be identified with Simeon and Levi's murderous attack on the people of Shechem (Genesis 34:25-31).

When the Israelites settled in central Canaan, they buried Joseph's bones, which they had brought from Egypt, 'at Shechem, in the portion of ground which Jacob bought from the sons of Hamor, the father of Shechem, for a hundred pieces of money' (or, as the New English Bible has it, 'a hundred sheep'; compare Genesis 33:19); 'it became an inheritance of the descendants of Joseph' (Joshua 24:32). The tomb of Joseph is still pointed out; it is covered with a dome, like many other 'weli's', or monuments of holy men, in the Islamic world.

About 325 yards south-east of Joseph's tomb lies Jacob's well. As is usual with wells, springs and pools mentioned in the Bible, the authenticity of this well is as certain as anything of the kind can reasonably be. Although the Samaritan woman said that 'our father Jacob . . . gave us the well, and drank from it himself, and his sons, and his cattle' (John 4:12), there is no account of this in the Genesis narrative. The woman was probably repeating an ancient and reliable local tradition.

The pilgrim from Bordeaux who visited the place in AD 333 notes that 'some plane trees are there, planted by Jacob, and there is a bath which receives its water from this

Looking south-east from Mount Ebal to Mount Gerizim. Jesus followed the north-south route through the mountains from Galilee to Judea and Jerusalem, stopping at Jacob's Well where he met the Samaritan woman.

well.' Half a century later, a church building stood over the well; it was seen probably by the pilgrim Egeria in AD 381, and certainly by Jerome about AD 390. Seven centuries later the Crusaders built another church on the spot. Both in their turn were destroyed by Muslims. The site is now marked by an unfinished Orthodox church, begun early in the twentieth century. To approach the well head today one must go down into the crypt of this church; it is no longer exposed to sun and air, as it was in Jesus' day.

Two different Greek words are used for the well in John's Gospel: one means a well or cistern which is dug out (so as to receive and retain rain-water); the other means a natural spring. Both words are applicable to Jacob's well: it was dug, indeed, but 'is fed by an underground stream, which rarely gives out' (E.F.F. Bishop). The woman spoke truly when she said, 'the well is deep' (John 4:11). Even today it is said to be about 130 feet deep, and it was probably deeper then. Canon H.B. Tristram, a famous Palestinian explorer of the nineteenth century, is said on one occasion to have 'sat thus by the well' about midday and started to read the fourth chapter of John. As he read, he grew drowsy in the heat of the sun, and suddenly let his New Testament fall from his hands into the well. (At that time the well was not yet built over.) The book was recovered several years later, during an unusually dry winter.

The well stands near the ancient north-south road from Galilee to Judea through central Palestine. It was natural that Jesus, weary and hot with his journey, should turn off the road and sit at the well head, asking the favour of a drink from the first person who came to draw water. He does not appear to have troubled about the risk of his incurring ritual pollution: as the New English Bible correctly renders the last clause of John 4:9, 'Jews and Samaritans

Fields in Samaria are still ploughed with a single ploughshare drawn by a horse or a donkey. The land is mountainous with rocky soil; a contrast with fertile Galilee.

... do not use vessels in common'. But that he should engage in serious religious discussion with a woman, and a Samaritan woman at that, surprised his disciples when they rejoined him.

The water in the well is still beautifully refreshing, even if it remains true that 'every one who drinks of this water will thirst again' (John 4:13).

'This mountain' on which, as the woman said, 'our fathers worshipped' (John 4:20), is Mount Gerizim, which rises on the south to a height of 2,900 feet above Mediterranean sea level and 700 feet above the pass lying between it and Mount Ebal on the north. (Mount Ebal is rather higher, about 3,077 feet above Mediterranean sea level). Gerizim is still to the Samaritan community the holiest place on earth, chosen by the Lord out of all the tribes of Israel 'to put his name and make his habitation there' (Deuteronomy 12:5).

The site of the 'city' of Sychar is disputed. Two miles to the west is the modern city of Nablus, perpetuating the name of Flavia Neapolis, founded by the Roman Emperor Vespasian in AD 72. Immediately to the south of Joseph's tomb is Tell Balatah, marking the site of the Old Testament Shechem. The Old Syriac version of the Gospels translated Sychar as Shechem, and Jerome thought that Sychar was a corruption of Shechem; but the Greek text makes a clear distinction between Sychar and Shechem (*Sychem* in Greek). Sychar has been commonly identified with the village of 'Askar, less than a mile north of Jacob's well. This identification may be correct, although no reliance should be placed on the similarity of name, for *'askar* is an Arabic term for a military camp, and would not be known in Palestine before the Arab conquest of the seventh century AD. But three hundred years and more before the Arab conquest Eusebius of Caesarea (about AD 325) and the Bordeaux pilgrim (AD 333) distinguish Sychar from the ruined Shechem and the inhabited Neapolis. The Bordeaux pilgrim says that Sychar lay a Roman mile distant from Shechem. It appears, then, that the name Sychar was known in the fourth century and is quite independent of the Arabic word *'askar*, although that Arabic word was later given as a name to the place earlier known as Sychar.

The Talmud twice mentions a spring called 'Ain Soker, which may be identical with the plentiful fountain still existing in

Jacob's Well is fed by an underground stream, and in Jesus' time was also a cistern to collect rainwater.

MEDITERRANEAN SEA

● Sebaste

● Sychar

▷ Mount Gerizim

Jericho● *River Jordan*

● Jerusalem
● ● Bethany

Valley floors are sown with corn and vegetables, while olive trees grow on the terraced slopes.

'Askar. If so, the Hebrew name of Sychar was Soker. (Some centuries before that, about 100 BC, the *Book of Jubilees* mentions a place in the Shechem area called Sakir.) If the town from which the woman came occupied the site of modern 'Askar, she would have passed the fountain 'Ain Soker and also crossed a stream on her way to Jacob's well; but perhaps she preferred not to join her neighbours in drawing water from the sources which they frequented.

Biblical references John 4:5
This is the only place in the Bible where Sychar is mentioned, but the conversation at the wellhead has immortalised the name of the place. A nineteenth-century devotional writer, John Gifford Bellett, is said to have died with the words on his lips: 'Oh, the Man of Sychar!' That such a rare place-name should be used to supply our Lord with a very fitting designation bears witness to the impact of this chapter.
John 4:20-26
Had we been in Jesus' place we should probably have told the Samaritan woman that she needed to be born again, and discussed the nature of true worship with Nicodemus. Why did he do it the other way round?
John 4:38
'Others have laboured.' Who were they? Aenon and Salim, where John the Baptist and his disciples ministered for a short time (John 3:23), were in the same region as Sychar. Perhaps it was into their labour that the disciples of Jesus had now entered.

Jericho

Jericho plays a notable part in the gospel narrative of Jesus' last journey to Jerusalem. It is here that he gave blind Bartimaeus the power to see, here too that he invited himself to be a guest in the house of Zacchaeus, the chief tax-collector of the district (Luke 18:35–19:10).

No doubt Jesus had visited Jericho on several earlier occasions. The traditional site of his baptism in the Jordan is about five miles to the east; Mount Quarantana,

the traditional place of his forty days' fast and temptation, rises to the north-west (due west of Tell es-Sultan). The old road down from Jerusalem (2,500 feet above Mediterranean sea level) to Jericho (820 feet below), descending well over 3,500 feet in some fifteen miles, follows the course of the Wadi Qilt; this road was the scene of the 'mugging' which features in the parable of the good Samaritan. The courtyard of the Inn of the Good Samaritan marks the sup-

The site of Old Testament Jericho, Tell es-Sultan, near Elisha's fountain.

Jericho is an oasis in the hot, dusty Jordan rift valley, 820 feet below sea-level. In Jesus' time, groves of palm and balsam trees yielded lucrative crops.

posed site of the place where the injured man was lodged and tended (Luke 10:30-35).

The Jericho that Jesus knew lay nearly two miles south of the Old Testament Jericho. The site of Old Testament Jericho – the city destroyed by Joshua and rebuilt 400 years later by Hiel the Bethelite (1 Kings 16:34) – is marked by the mound called Tell es-Sultan, near Elisha's fountain ('Ain es-Sultan), the perennial spring whose plentiful water-supply of 1,000 gallons a minute irrigates the whole surrounding countryside and makes it a place of palm-trees, gardens and plantations.

New Testament Jericho, represented by the ruins called Tulul Abu el-'Alayiq, had its beginnings in the period following the return from the Babylonian exile. The Hellenistic rulers erected a fortress here to guard the road from the Jordan to Jerusalem. Bacchides, a general of the

Seleucid kingdom who waged war with Judas Maccabaeus, added further fortifications about 160 BC, and the early Hasmonaean rulers continued these operations. It was at Jericho that Simon the Hasmonaean high priest, last surviving brother of Judas Maccabaeus, was assassinated by his son-in-law in 134 BC.

The importance of Jericho economically as well as strategically was, if anything, enhanced under the Roman occupation, from 63 BC onwards. The presence of a chief tax-collector in Jericho in the time of Jesus is not at all surprising: the city commanded the main road from Transjordan into Judea. Herod the Great (37-4 BC) constructed a series of fortresses around the area to protect it, and augmented its water-supply by a system of aqueducts bringing water from other sources than Elisha's fountain (always the principal source). He built a new city on both sides of the Wadi Qilt, after the style of contemporary Italian cities, in which lavish use was made of *opus reticulatum* (in which lozenge-shaped pieces of stone were set in concrete). Herodian Jericho, in fact, resembled a more extensive Pompeii. It contained public buildings, amphitheatre, hippodrome, gymnasium or palaestra (wrestling arena), parks, gardens, pools and villas, and (most impressive of all) a luxuriously appointed winter palace. It was here that Herod died in 4 BC.

Jericho suffered damage by fire in the disorders which broke out after Herod's death, but was soon restored by his son Archelaus. It was taken, but not destroyed, by Vespasian in AD 68, when, as commander-in-chief of the Roman forces in Judea, he was engaged in suppressing the Jewish revolt. It has been thought that about the same time some of his troops attacked and destroyed the Essene settlement at Qumran, about eight miles south of Jericho, on the north-west shore of the Dead Sea. Vespasian, having captured

Jericho, stationed large bodies of soldiers there in preparation for his attack on Jerusalem. When the second Jewish revolt against the Romans broke out in AD 132, under the leadership of Bar-kokhba, Jericho was again fortified by the Romans and served as a centre from which insurgent outposts in the wilderness of Judea were reduced.

After the suppression of the revolt in AD 135, the importance of Jericho began to decline. The Bordeaux pilgrim visited the city in AD 333 and was shown the sycamore tree which Zacchaeus climbed. (Jerome also refers to the sycamore over half a century later; so does Peter the Deacon, of Monte Cassino, who wrote a book on the holy places about 1137, during the period of Crusader rule). Whatever may be thought of the genuineness of the sycamore, there is no doubt about Elisha's fountain, which the Bordeaux pilgrim also saw: it is one and a

Herod built a system of aqueducts to augment the supply of fresh water.

New Testament Jericho lay about two miles south of Tell es-Sultan. The city Jesus knew had been richly developed by Herod the Great in Roman style, and included a luxurious winter palace.

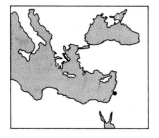

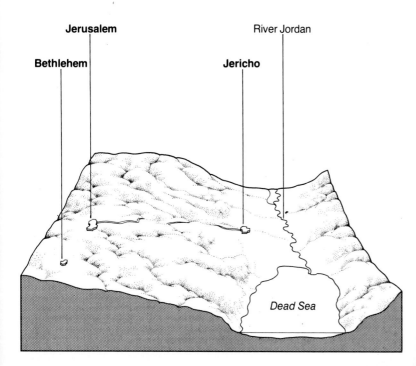

Bethlehem

Jerusalem

Jericho

River Jordan

Dead Sea

half Roman miles from Roman Jericho, he says, adding that any woman who drinks from it will have children – thanks to Elisha's healing of the water with salt (2 Kings 2:19-22). He was shown the house of Rahab standing above the spring: whoever showed him this must be given credit at least for knowing that Old Testament Jericho stood in that neighbourhood, some distance from Roman Jericho.

Not long after the Bordeaux pilgrim's visit Roman Jericho was deserted. A new city was founded in Byzantine times about a mile to the east of it; it is on the site of the Byzantine city that modern Jericho stands – still, like its Old Testament predecessor, 'the city of palm trees' (Deuteronomy 34:3).

The isolated Inn of the Good Samaritan on the narrow old Jerusalem–Jericho road brings to mind Jesus' parable.

Biblical references Luke 18:35-19:10

Jericho in the Old Testament is the city of the curse – but not invariably so. There was a school of prophets there (2 Kings 2:5), and they do not appear to have been troubled by the thought that they were living on accursed ground. Elisha healed the water of the spring there (2 Kings 2:21), so the blessing of God proved more powerful than the curse of Joshua 6:26. And when Jesus came to Jericho, nothing but blessing attended his visit: Bartimaeus received his sight and Zacchaeus was made a new man, for, as Jesus proclaimed there of all places, 'the Son of man came to seek and to save the lost' – to turn the curse into a blessing.

The house of a wealthy Palestinian family in the time of Jesus.

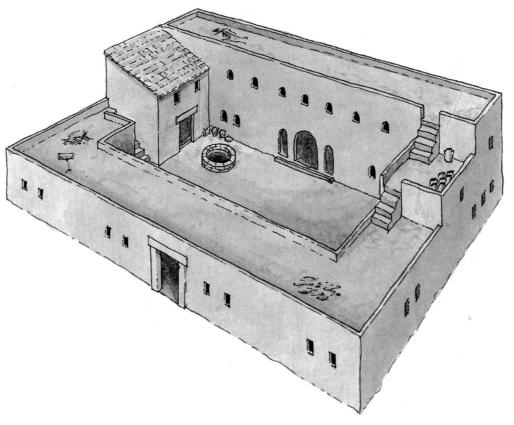

Bethany

Bethany is best known in the gospel story as the home of Mary, Martha and Lazarus. Luke does not give us the name of the 'village' where Martha (evidently the older sister) 'received Jesus into her house', but it must have been Bethany, if John's record is allowed to shed light on Luke's. Here Mary sat at Jesus' feet and listened to his teaching while Martha was busily engaged in preparing a meal for the honoured guest (Luke 10:38-42). Here, later, Lazarus their brother fell ill and died, and was raised to life by Jesus (John 11:1-44). Here Jesus was guest of honour at a meal during Holy Week, 'in the house of Simon the leper' (Mark 14:3; compare John 12:2), and was anointed with costly nard by a woman whom John identifies as Mary. Later, after he was raised from the dead, Jesus led his disciples out 'as far as Bethany' and took his leave of them (Luke 24:50, 51; compare Acts 1:9-12).

Looking west from the Inn of the Good Samaritan, the Mount of Olives is silhouetted against the dusk. Bethany is on the eastern slope of the mount; Jerusalem lies less than two miles away to the west.

Bethany lies on the eastern slope of the Mount of Olives, less than two miles from Jerusalem (John 11:18). The meaning of the name is uncertain: if it is an abbreviation of Beth-Ananiah (the house of Ananiah), it may be the Ananiah of Nehemiah 11:32. Bethany, as such, first appears in literature in Judith 1:9, where it is mentioned alongside Jerusalem. It was the last staging-post on the road from Jericho to Jerusalem.

The Bordeaux pilgrim visited Bethany in AD 333 and was shown the vault or crypt in which the body of Lazarus was believed to have lain. Eusebius of Caesarea mentions the vault or crypt around the same time. Not long afterwards a church was built over the site, for Egeria saw it in AD 381: she tells how a special service was held there towards the end of Lent, 'six days before the Passover' (compare John 12:1). It is from this church, called the Lazareion (or shrine of Lazarus), that the Muslim name of the village, El-Azariyeh, is derived. The

Muslims of Bethany regard Lazarus as a saint. Egeria saw another church half a mile on the Jerusalem side of the Lazareion, at the reported spot where Mary met the Lord as he was on his way to the tomb of Lazarus (John 11:29) – an improbable site, because Jesus on this occasion came to Bethany from the Jordan, not from Jerusalem.

Excavations conducted in Bethany between 1949 and 1953 uncovered remains of four churches, the later ones built over the earlier ones, to the east of the traditional tomb of Lazarus. The earliest of the four may have been the church seen by Egeria. Mosaics from all of them could be distinguished. In their precincts and vicinity were many rock-cut tombs. The most recent of these four churches was transformed into a mosque, which still stands.

The visitor to Bethany today is shown an opening in the hillside leading into the underground chamber traditionally held to be the tomb of Lazarus. Some fifty feet lower down, the modern Franciscan Church of St. Lazarus was built in 1953, on the supposed site of Martha's house. It is beautifully decorated with murals depicting relevant scenes from the gospel narrative. Some interesting relics are housed in it, including a mosaic from the sixth-century Byzantine church which once stood there, and a Roman inscription bearing witness to the presence nearby of the Tenth (Fretensian) Legion, the military unit which occupied Judea after the fall of

Jesus spent the week before his last Passover in Bethany, staying in the house of Simon the Leper.

An intricate mosaic from the Byzantine church near Lazarus' tomb.

The entrance to the stone crypt where Lazarus may have been laid before Jesus brought him back to life.

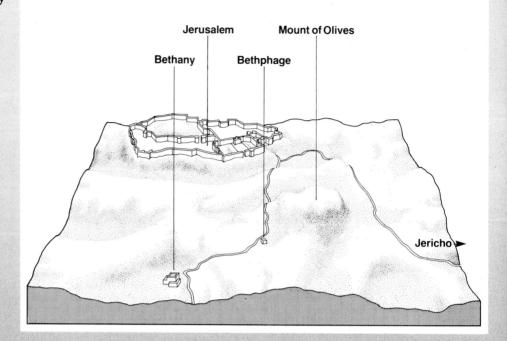

Bethany   Jerusalem   Bethphage   Mount of Olives   Jericho

Jerusalem in AD 70.

The old road from Bethany to Jerusalem, crossing the summit of the Mount of Olives, passed by Bethphage (meaning 'the place of figs'). This was the village where the disciples found the donkey ready tethered for Jesus' use and brought it to their master, in accordance with his instructions, so that he might complete his journey to Jerusalem on its back (Mark 11:1-10). It is frequently suggested that the present village of Et-Tur, on the summit, stands where Bethphage stood. This may well be so. The small Franciscan church marking the spot where Jesus is held to have mounted the donkey stands some way down the eastern slope, on the Bethany side of Et-Tur, but Jesus is not said to have mounted the donkey at Bethphage: the disciples brought it from the village to the point which Jesus had reached on his way from Bethany. From this church a procession to Jerusalem starts every Palm Sunday. A similar procession is described by Egeria in AD 384, except that in her day it set out from the church called Eleona (built by the Emperor Constantine on the summit to commemorate the Ascension). The procession, as it moves down the western slope of the hill, passes the church called Dominus Flevit ('The Lord wept'), marking the spot where Jesus came in sight of Jerusalem and wept over it (Luke 19:41). The dome of the church has the shape of a tear-drop, and in front of the little altar within there is a mosaic depicting a hen gathering her chickens under her wings (compare Matthew 23:37).

Looking from the Mount of Olives across old Jerusalem at sunrise. Walls once enclosed the magnificent Temple built by Herod the Great.

Biblical references Luke 10:38-42
The village is not named, but comparison with John's record leaves us in no doubt that it was Bethany. Here we are introduced to the two sisters and their respective activities when Jesus visited them: Martha waiting on him and Mary learning from him.
John 11:1-44
That Jesus is the resurrection and the life is declared in word and shown in action at Bethany.
Mark 11:11
After the excitement in Jerusalem day by day during Holy Week, Bethany provides welcome rest by night.
Mark 14:3-9; John 12:1-8
The supper party at Bethany provides a setting for the anointing of Jesus. At least one person recognises his royal dignity. The costliness of the ointment is emphasised: nothing but the best is good enough for the King of kings. And when we are tempted to say, 'This might have been sold for a large sum, and given to the poor,' let us reflect who it was that first said it.
Luke 24:50,51
Bethany is here the scene of the final blessing and parting.

Ancient olive trees flourish in a garden on the slopes where Jesus and his disciples met in the Garden of Gethsemane.

Jerusalem

The 'Synoptic Gospels' (Matthew, Mark, Luke) tell of only one visit by Jesus to Jerusalem, the visit during which he was arrested, put on trial and crucified – except for Luke's account of his being taken there in his infancy and later at the age of twelve (Luke 2:22-50). John, on the other hand, tells of several occasions when he visited Jerusalem in the course of his ministry, especially at some of the great feasts of the Jewish year (John 2:13; 5:1; 7:10; 10:22;

12:12). It would be surprising if he had not paid repeated visits to Jerusalem, and indeed the Synoptic record suggests that he did visit it several times, when he is reported as addressing the city: 'How often would I have gathered your children together...' (Luke 13:34). Even if, as some think, these words are quoted from a 'wisdom' saying, they would not have been relevant unless they had expressed his own experience.

The Jerusalem that Jesus knew was small

The Dome of the Rock is the most prominent building in modern Jerusalem.

in scope but impressive in appearance. Its status as a holy city had been confirmed to it by successive Gentile overlords – Persian, Greek and Roman. Jesus called it 'the city of the great King' (Matthew 5:35), quoting Psalm 48:2. Whether the psalmist was referring to God or to a king of David's line, there is no doubt that on Jesus' lips 'the great King' was God. In Jewish belief, Jerusalem was the city which the God of Israel had chosen 'to put his name and make his habitation there' (Deuteronomy 12:5). By Jesus' day it had changed almost beyond recognition from the city that was hurriedly rebuilt by the impoverished Jews who returned from the Babylonian exile in 539 BC and the following years.

The main quarters of the city, however, remained much as they had been before: they were determined largely by natural features. The city was divided into two parts by the north-south line of the Tyropoeon Valley (the Valley of the Cheesemakers). East of that valley stood the Temple and associated buildings; south of the Temple stood the lower city, the eastern section of which (Ophel) was the original Jerusalem which David captured from the Jebusites and chose as his own capital (2 Samuel 5:6-9). West of the Tyropoeon Valley was the upper city, which does not appear to have been settled so early as the lower city. The south-west quarter was evidently first occupied during the Judean monarchy: it may have been the 'Second Quarter' in

which the prophetess Huldah lived about 621 BC (2 Kings 22:14).

Perhaps eighty years after the return from exile, an abortive attempt was made to surround the city with a wall (Ezra 4:12). The building of a wall was actually carried through by Nehemiah, in accordance with the decree of Artaxerxes I, king of Persia (445 BC). Nehemiah's wall probably enclosed the lower city and the south-western quarter. The Temple was separately enclosed. On the north, the wall probably followed the west-east line of the present King David Street, running north of the south-western quarter and crossing the Tyropoeon Valley to meet the western wall of the Temple.

The walls of Jerusalem were repaired by the high priest Simon II about 200 BC but they were broken down in 167 BC by Antiochus Epiphanes, who built a strong citadel in the city of David, south of the Temple. The city was refortified by the Hasmonaeans, especially by John Hyrcanus (1 Maccabees 16:23).

Jerusalem was greatly beautified by Herod the Great, who erected or restored many fine buildings. Apart from the Temple, the most magnificent of all his buildings (see p.58), he rebuilt the fortress of Baris, north-west of the Temple area, and renamed it Antonia, after his patron Mark Antony; he built a palace for himself on the west wall of the city ('Herod's praetorium' of Acts 23:35) and three strong

Vegetable stalls under the cool arches of a covered market. The narrow streets of the Old City are lined with small shops selling food and handicrafts.

towers in its neighbourhood, one of which is incorporated in the present Citadel. He also built such public installations as an amphitheatre and a hippodrome. It was under Herod, if not earlier, that a second north wall was built to enclose the north-western quarter of the city: it began at an unidentified point called the Gate Gennath and ran in a northerly and then easterly direction, passing south of the present Church of the Holy Sepulchre, until it reached the Antonia fortress. The area of the walled city that Jesus knew was about half a square mile (320 acres); its population may have been as high as 50,000. But already people were beginning to build dwelling-houses beyond the second north wall, in the section called Bezetha or Newtown; between ten and fifteen years after the death of Jesus, Herod's grandson Herod Agrippa I ('Herod the king' of Acts 12:1) began to build a third north wall to

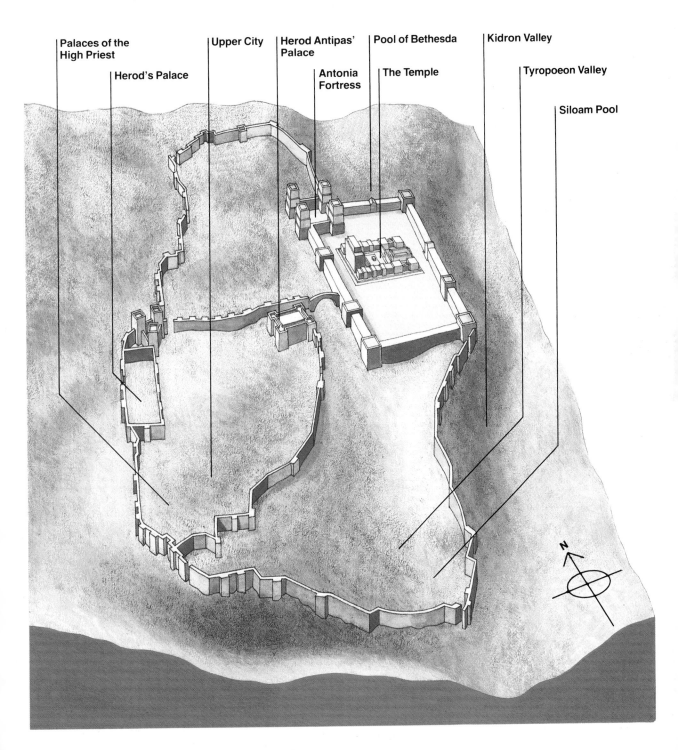

Palaces of the High Priest

Herod's Palace

Upper City

Herod Antipas' Palace

Antonia Fortress

Pool of Bethesda

The Temple

Kidron Valley

Tyropoeon Valley

Siloam Pool

Jerusalem

enclose this suburb. After the destruction of the city by Titus in AD 70, it lay derelict for over sixty years. Then the Roman Emperor Hadrian founded a new, completely Gentile, city on the site and called it Aelia Capitolina (AD 135); the walls which enclosed it are followed substantially by the present walls of the Old City.

Some of the sites in Jerusalem mentioned in the gospel story, especially by John, can be identified with confidence; others are more doubtful. The pools of Bethesda and Siloam can be located with certainty. At Bethesda, north of the Temple area, near the present Church of St. Anne, there were twin pools which received water from a nearby source of supply. Four porticoes enclosed the area of the two pools, while a fifth stood on the ridge which separated the two. The first reference to Bethesda outside the New Testament comes in the copper scroll found in Cave 3 at Qumran; it calls the place by its Hebrew name Beth-esdathain, 'the place of two outpourings'. To the water, with its reddish tinge, healing properties were ascribed, but the disabled man who had waited his turn for so long in one of the porticoes might have waited for the rest of his life if Jesus had not come along and healed him promptly and effectively (John 5:1-9).

The pool of Siloam, at the southern end of the Tyropoeon Valley, near its junction with the Valley of Hinnom (south of the

The Garden Tomb gives an impression of the scene of Jesus' resurrection.

city) and the Kidron Valley (east of the city), receives the water which flows through a tunnel cut through the rock from the Virgin's Fountain (the spring Gihon of the Old Testament) in the Kidron Valley, east of the city of David. The tunnel, a piece of skilled engineering work, whose construction was commemorated in a Hebrew inscription cut in the rock near its exit, is usually identified with that undertaken at the command of King Hezekiah in 701 BC (2 Kings 20:20; 2 Chronicles 32:4; Isaiah 22:9). When John reports how Jesus sent the blind man whose eyes he had smeared with clay to go to the pool of Siloam and wash it off, he mentions that Siloam means 'sent' (John 9:7). This name

(Shiloah in Isaiah 8:6) referred to the 'sending' of the water from the spring Gihon through the tunnel into the pool; but John reflects that true spiritual sight is imparted only through faith in him who has been 'sent' by God.

The Mount of Olives, to the east of the city, across the Kidron, is of course an undisputed biblical site. The garden where 'Jesus often met with his disciples' (John 18:2) – called Gethsemane in the Synoptic Gospels – was on the western slope of Olivet: its location is not known for sure, but it cannot have been far from the traditional site marked by the Church of All Nations and other commemorative buildings. The Franciscans maintain a garden in

Old Jerusalem from the road to Bethlehem, looking northwest. The Mount of Olives rises to the east of the walls, over the Kidron Valley.

the immediate vicinity; some of the olives in it may be up to 1,000 years old. The Church of Eleona (i.e. Olivet) was built by Constantine on the summit of the hill to enclose a cave where Jesus was believed to have instructed the inner circle of his disciples. The Bordeaux pilgrim saw the church when he visited Palestine in AD 333. This was also the first place where the ascension of Jesus was commemorated by Christians. But about AD 390 a noble lady named Poemenia founded a colonnade a little way off, called the Holy Ascension, surrounding the rock from which some believed Jesus to have ascended into heaven. On this site there now stands a circular domed building. It is under Muslim guardianship, but Christians are permitted to hold an Ascension Day service there. The rock is still to be seen inside the building; the custodians point out a depression in it, in shape not unlike a human footprint, which they say was made by one of Jesus' feet immediately before he ascended.

No great certainty attaches to some of the sites recalling episodes in the passion narrative, such as the Cenacle (the house where the Last Supper was eaten) or the Church of St. Peter in Gallicantu, said to stand where the high priest's palace stood. For the place where Jesus appeared before Pilate there are two rival sites. The place is called the praetorium in Mark 15:16 and John 18:28,33; this word denotes the headquarters of the governor or commanding officer, and in the context of the trial narrative it might refer either to the Antonia fortress or to Herod's palace. Beneath the Convent of the Sisters of Zion, which stands more or less where the Antonia fortress did, may be seen a Roman pavement which has been identified with the Pavement of John 19:13, where Pilate pronounced judgement on Jesus. The lines of the soldiers' 'game of the king' are traced out on one part of the pavement; this, it is suggested, may be the very spot where they dressed Jesus up in mock-royal robes and hailed him as King of the Jews. In the opinion of some reputable archaeologists, however, this pavement, like the Ecce Homo arch visible in the street above, dates back only to Hadrian's time. If the Antonia fortress was indeed the praetorium of the Gospels, then the present line of the Via Dolorosa corresponds more or less to the actual road on which Jesus was led to the cross – only several feet higher. If the praetorium was Herod's palace, then the actual way to the cross must have been quite different from the traditional one.

The place of crucifixion was outside the city gate (Hebrews 13:12). The Church of the Holy Sepulchre, which traditionally marks the site of Jesus' death, burial and resurrection, stood just outside the second north wall. The memory of the site was preserved, even after Hadrian had enclosed it within his own north wall and erected a pagan temple there. It was because of the persistence of the Christian tradition that Constantine, about AD 325, removed the

Jesus sent a blind man to the Pool of Siloam to wash clay from his eyes and receive his sight.

pagan installations and brought to light the holy sepulchre. The Bordeaux pilgrim visited the place while Constantine's basilica was being built, and mentions the rock outcrop called Golgotha 'where the Lord was crucified, and about a stone's throw from it the vault where they laid his body, and from which he rose again on the third day'. Constantine's basilica, the Church of the Holy Sepulchre (consecrated about AD 335), was originally and more happily called the Anastasis or 'Resurrection' (it is so called by Egeria fifty years after its consecration).

It calls for a powerful effort of the imagination for the visitor to the church today to envisage the site as it was in Jesus' time. Many visitors get a better impression of what it looked like from the Garden Tomb, off the Nablus road. Here we have a garden containing a tomb, like that described in John 19:41, although it cannot be seriously claimed that this is the historical site. The suggestion that it was so goes back to 1883, when the identification formed part of General Gordon's fancy that Jerusalem was laid out on the plan of a human body, with Calvary or Golgotha, 'the place of a skull', corresponding to the head. It is sufficient to reflect that, whatever place is pointed out as Jesus' tomb, 'he is not here, for he has risen'.

Biblical references Matthew 4:5
Jerusalem is here called 'the holy city'; yet in Matthew 23:37 it is charged with 'killing the prophets and stoning those who are sent to you!' In Matthew 5:35 it is 'the city of the great King'; in Revelation 11:8 it is 'the great city which is allegorically called Sodom and Egypt, where their Lord was crucified'. A strange set of contradictions, one might think. What really makes a city holy?

The Church of the Holy Sepulchre stands over a site outside the contemporary city wall, near where Jesus died and rose again.

The Temple

Part of the Western Wall of Herod's Temple and Wilson's Arch. The arches were part of a viaduct which linked the upper city with the Temple, across the Tyropoeon Valley.

When Jesus had completed his journey on Palm Sunday, 'he entered Jerusalem, and went into the Temple; and when he had looked round at everything, as it was already late, he went out to Bethany with the twelve' (Mark 11:11).

The Temple Jesus knew was the Temple renovated, enlarged and beautified by Herod the Great. Architecturally it was new; religiously it was still Zerubbabel's Temple, rebuilt after the Jews returned from the Babylonian exile. The six centuries between the return from exile and the destruction of Jerusalem in AD 70 are known in Jewish history as the age of the Second Temple.

The site on which the Temple stood had sacred associations reaching back to ancient times: according to tradition, the rock which crops out on the top of the Temple hill was the place where Abraham built the altar to sacrifice Isaac – 'one of the moun-

Porticos

Court of the Gentiles

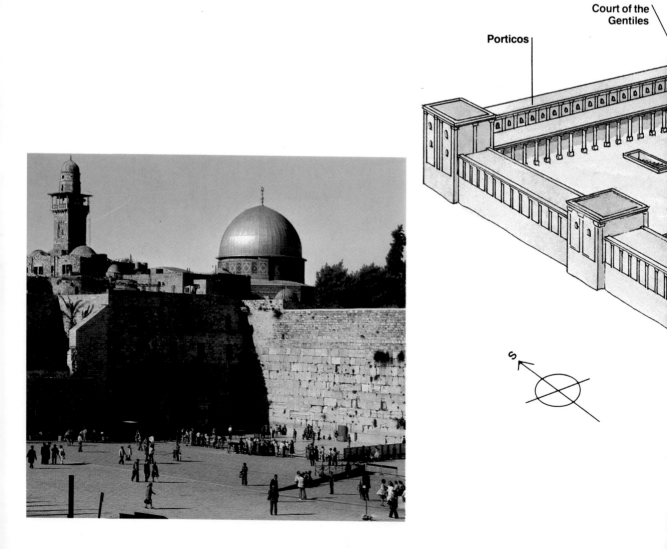

tains' in 'the land of Moriah' (Genesis 22:2) being identified with 'Mount Moriah' (2 Chronicles 3:1).

Solomon's Temple had stood on the site for over 350 years when it was destroyed by the Babylonians (587 BC) beyond the possibility of repair. About seventy years later a completely new Temple was built there, by authorisation of the Persian king. When it was dedicated on March 12, 515 BC, some very old people who could remember Solomon's Temple reckoned it a poor thing in comparison with its magnificent predecessor. Yet the contemporary prophet Haggai predicted far greater glory for it in days to come (Haggai 2:3-9). The high priesthood in the new Temple remained for nearly 350 years in the family of Zadok, which had supplied the chief priests in Solomon's Temple from its dedication onwards.

The Temple was repaired, extended and adorned at various times between Zerubbabel and Herod. One man who is credited with a distinguished contribution to this work is Simon II, high priest about 200 BC: among other things, he fortified the Temple precincts with a surrounding wall. A few decades after his time the Temple suffered a major – but, mercifully, short-lived – disaster when, in the days of the Maccabees, it was turned over by the persecuting king Antiochus Epiphanes to the worship of a pagan deity, scornfully referred to by the Jews as 'the abomination of desolation' (1 Maccabees 1:54). This desecration lasted for exactly three years: the regaining and re-consecration of the Temple by Judas Maccabaeus in December 164 BC, has been commemorated ever since by Hanukkah, the Jewish Feast of the Dedication. In John 10:22 Jesus is said to have walked in the Temple courts during this feast less than four months before his death.

None of the restorations or extensions of the second Temple could match, however,

An artist's impression of Herod's Temple.

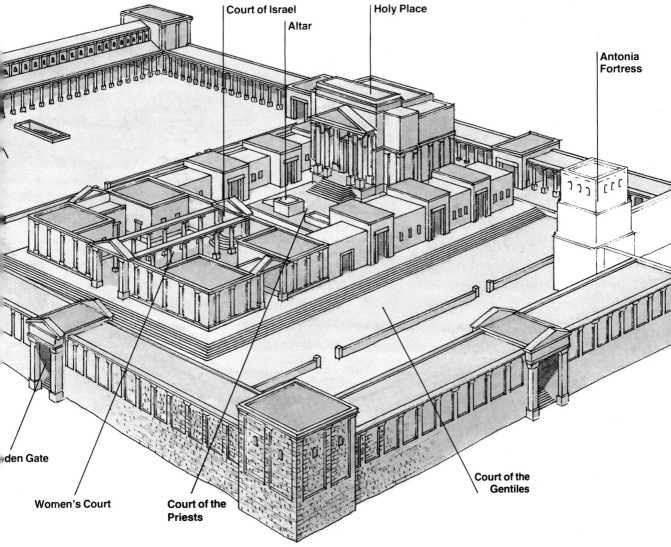

Court of Israel

Altar

Holy Place

Antonia Fortress

den Gate

Women's Court

Court of the Priests

Court of the Gentiles

with the work initiated by Herod at the beginning of 19 BC. Because certain parts of the building could not be entered by the laity, a thousand Levites were specially trained as builders and masons, and carried out their work so efficiently and carefully that at no time was there any interruption in the sacrifices and other services. The Temple platform was extended eastwards on vaulted foundations, with strong retaining walls, so as to increase the area of the precincts, especially of the outer court. The courts were enclosed by magnificent colonnades. Along the east side of the outer court ran what was called Solomon's Colonnade; it was here that Jesus was seen walking during the Feast of the Dedication. Before long it became a habitual meeting-place for the infant church (see Acts 3:11; 5:12).

Wealthy Jews of the dispersion (that is, those living outside Palestine) sent costly offerings to enhance the splendour of the place. For example, the Beautiful Gate of Acts 3:2, 10 is generally identified with the magnificent gate of Corinthian bronze presented by an Alexandrian Jew named Nicanor (after whom it is also called the Nicanor Gate). It probably stood at the top of the steps leading up from the outer court to the Court of the Women.

While the main part of Herod's rebuilding was completed before his death in 4 BC, the work went on for more than sixty years after that. When Jesus visited the Temple at the first passover of his ministry it was remarked that the place had by then been forty-six years under construction. The work was not entirely finished until AD 63, only seven years before the destruction of the whole fabric.

We are fortunate in having an eyewitness account of Herod's Temple from Josephus, who was born into a priestly family of Jerusalem in AD 37. He was thus well acquainted with the Temple in the days of its greatest architectural glory and was present with the Roman forces when it was burned in AD 70. Another detailed description, preserved in the tradition of the rabbinical schools, was finally set down in writing about AD 200, in a tractate of the Mishnah (the authoritative compilation of Jewish oral law) called *Middoth* ('measurements').

The whole area was holy, but it became increasingly holy as one penetrated farther in, from east to west. The outer court, enclosed by Herod with colonnades, is sometimes referred to as the Court of the Gentiles because non-Jews (like the Greeks of John 12:20) were permitted to enter it and walk about in it. But they were forbidden to go into any of the inner courts: notices in Greek and Latin gave warning that the penalty for such trespass was death. The Romans permitted the Jewish authorities to pass the death-sentence for this offence and to carry it out, even if the offender were a Roman citizen. It was for allegedly aiding and abetting an offence of this kind that Paul was attacked and nearly beaten to death by an angry crowd during his last visit to Jerusalem (Acts 21:27-32).

The inner courts were on a higher level than the outer court: one had to go up several steps to get into them. The easternmost of the inner courts was the Court of the Women – so called because Jewish women were admitted thus far (but no farther). In this court, at the west end, was the 'treasury', the section where there stood thirteen trumpet-shaped containers for voluntary offerings of money. Jesus was sitting 'opposite the treasury' when he saw the widow put into one of the containers the two 'mites' which were all that she had (Mark 12:41-44).

Beyond that was the Court of Israel, which was open to Jewish laymen. The innermost court was the Court of the Priests, normally barred to all laymen. In the eastern part of this court, opposite the main gates leading from the other courts and the eastern entrance into the Temple precincts, so that it could be seen from a distance, stood the great altar of burnt-offering. At its west side stood the sanctuary proper, comprising (from east to west) the porch, the holy place, and the cubical holy of holies. Into the holy place the priests entered to discharge various duties, in particular to offer incense on the golden incense-altar, as Zechariah did on the occasion when an angel appeared to him and announced the forthcoming birth of his son John the Baptist (Luke 1:8-23). No ordinary priest could hope that the lot for offering the incense would fall to him on more than one day in his lifetime (if that); the day when Zechariah received the angelic announcement was in any case the red-letter day of his whole priestly career. Into the holy of holies only the high priest was allowed to go, and that but once a year, on the Day of Atonement in the autumn, when he presented sacrificial blood to expiate his own sins and those of the nation which he represented (Leviticus 16:1-34). In the Letter to the Hebrews this ritual is used as a parable (by contrast more than by comparison) of Jesus' atoning death and his present high-priestly ministry in the heavenly sanctuary. But during his Palestinian ministry Jesus, as a layman, could not go beyond the Court of Israel: 'if he were on earth, he would not be a priest at all' (Hebrews 8:4).

Herod's Temple and its precincts covered an area of twenty-six acres. (The *Haram esh-Sharif*, or 'Noble Enclosure', which occupies the same site today, covers thirty-five acres.) The walls surrounding the area provided it with a system of fortification quite distinct from that of the city. Part of Herod's walls, built of the huge stones which characterised his work, may be seen today: the most famous part is the Western Wall (formerly known as the Wailing Wall), the most sacred place of prayer in the Jewish world. The walls were pierced by several gates: there were four on the Western Wall, leading down into the Tyropoeon Valley (see p. 52). From the Western Wall also a viaduct was carried on arches across the valley to the upper city on the west: the pier of the easternmost arch is still to be seen springing from the Western Wall (it is known as Wilson's Arch, after Sir Charles Wilson, a British archaeologist of the nineteenth century). Farther south the remains of another arch can be seen springing from the Western Wall: this arch (Robinson's Arch, after the American pioneer explorer Edward Robinson) carried the first stage of a staircase which then turned south and led down to the main street. The staircase connected at the top with the Royal Colonnade or Royal Stoa, a covered gallery running along the whole southern side of the outer court and described by Josephus as a structure 'more noteworthy than any other under the sun'.

Jesus' first contact with the Temple was in his early infancy, when he was taken there for the ceremony of purification and was hailed as the coming Deliverer by Simeon and Anna (Luke 2:22-38). His next

The Western Wall; most sacred place of prayer in the Jewish world.

recorded visit to it was at the age of twelve, when – perhaps to prepare him for his Bar Mitzvah confirmation the following year – he was taken there at Passover time by Mary and Joseph and was found in conversation with the rabbis who had their 'teaching pitches' in the outer court (Luke 2:41-51).

The day was to come when Jesus himself, on successive visits to Jerusalem, would be a familiar figure as he taught in the outer court. Several of his discourses reported in the Gospel of John were delivered there – possibly the discourse on resurrection and judgment which followed the healing of the man at the pool of Bethesda (John 5:19-47) and certainly the discourses at the Feast of Tabernacles (John 7:14-8:58), at the Feast of Dedication (John 10:22-39) and during the week before the last Passover (John 12:30-36, 44-50).

It is there that the scene of the adulterous woman is set (John 8:2-11). It was there, too, that a challenge to Jesus' authority was answered with his parable of the vineyard, and that he dealt with the question about paying tribute to Caesar, refuted the Sadducees' objection against the doctrine of resurrection, gave a ruling on the two great commandments of the law and asked the scribes how the Messiah, being David's lord, could be his son (Mark 11:27-12:37).

Jesus' cleansing of the Temple is recorded in all four Gospels. John, perhaps because its implication for the replacement of the old order by a new one entitled it to a position in the forefront of Jesus' ministry, puts it in the context of an earlier visit to Jerusalem than the Synoptists do (compare John 2:13-22 with Matthew 21:12,13; Mark 11:15-18; Luke 19:45,46). It was in a section of the outer court that the vendors of sacrificial animals and the money-changers had set up their stalls and tables, and by doing so they encroached on its proper use. The outer court was the only part of the Temple area where Gentiles could draw near to the God of Israel; Jesus' action made more room for them, and his quotation of Isaiah 56:7, 'My house shall be called a house of prayer for all the nations' (Mark 11:17), suggests that he had their interests in mind. Those Greeks who had come to Jerusalem to worship God at the last Passover may have asked to see Jesus because they recognised that he had championed their spiritual interests (John 12:21).

The cleansing of the Temple was not the signal for a popular rising, although the Jewish authorities feared it might lead to that. It was rather a symbolical action like those sometimes performed by the Old Testament prophets to confirm their words. It is evident that no breach of the peace was involved, for there was no intervention by the Roman soldiers stationed in the adjoining Antonia fortress, north-west of the Temple area, which communicated with the outer court by two flights of steps (compare Acts 21:35, 40).

The interior of the golden dome over Mount Moriah, the site of Abraham's sacrifice.

The Dome of the Rock, Mosque of Omar, on the site of the Temple. Covering twenty-six acres, the Temple and its precincts were separately fortified from the city.

Jesus' last utterance about the Temple foretold its downfall. His disciples had been impressed by the magnificence of the structure, but as he sat with some of them on the slope of the Mount of Olives, looking across to the Temple area, he spoke of the time, not more than a generation distant, when not one stone would be left standing on another (Mark 13:2-30).

When Jesus was on trial before the high priest, an attempt was made to convict him of speaking against the Temple, but it failed because the witnesses gave conflicting evidence. Even so, people remembered what he was charged with saying, and when he was on the cross some passers-by mocked him as the one 'who would destroy the Temple and build it in three days' (Mark 15:29). 'But,' says John, the only evangelist who reports him as actually using such language, 'he spoke of the temple of his body' (John 2:21).

At the moment of Jesus' death, we are told, 'the curtain of the Temple was torn in two, from top to bottom' (Mark 15:38). If this was the curtain that hung before the holy of holies, the throne-room of the invisible presence of God, the incident seems to show that in the death of Jesus, God is fully revealed.

Biblical references Malachi 3:1
'The Lord whom you seek will suddenly come to his temple.' Many interpreters, especially in earlier days, have found the fulfilment of this prophecy in Jesus' cleansing of the Temple. Do you think this is likely? Consider the refining and purifying work which, in Malachi's prophecy, the Lord will undertake when he visits his Temple. Could Jesus' cleansing be described in these terms?
Mark 11:17
Jesus reminds his hearers how Isaiah had spoken of the Temple as 'a house of prayer for all the nations'. But that Temple had long since disappeared; is there anything to which the same description could be applied today?

The Western Wall under Wilson's Arch.

This relief from the Arch of Titus in Rome shows the Romans carrying off the seven-branched candlestick from the Temple after the fall of Jerusalem in AD 70.

Places Paul Knew

Three hundred years of peace prevailed throughout the Roman Empire from the time of the Emperor Augustus, with a few important exceptions. This allowed great freedom of travel throughout the Mediterranean world. Paul could travel along superb roads, and for most of his life look to the Roman government for protection.

ITALY

● Rome

ILLYRICUM & DALMATIA

MACEDONIA

Thessalonica

ACHAIA

MEDITERRANEAN SEA

Corinth ●
Athens ●

EGYPT

The Mediterranean

ESIA

ippi

THRACIA

BITHYNIA & PONTUS

ASIA

hesus

losse

GALATIA

CAPPADOCIA

LYCIA

Tarsus

CILICIA

Antioch

SYRIA

Damascus

Caesarea

Jerusalem

Introduction

Within a few years of Jesus' resurrection, the young church in Jerusalem, led by Peter and the apostles, was being persecuted by the Jewish religious leaders. Stephen's death, witnessed by a young Pharisee named Saul, is recorded by Luke in the Acts of the Apostles. This is the first time we meet the man who was to evangelise the Roman Empire.

Paul's conversion on the way to Damascus happened within a few years of Pentecost. After his encounter with the risen Christ, Paul visited Damascus briefly, spent some time in Arabia, modern Jordan, and visited Jerusalem two or three years later. He embarked at Caesarea for the sea-crossing to Tarsus, where he stayed for about ten years, preaching the gospel.

Paul started preaching and teaching in Tarsus not more than five years after Jesus' ascension. Within fifteen years he had gone to help Barnabas in Antioch, and from there Paul and Barnabas began their travels to Cyprus and Asia Minor. The gospel reached Macedonia within twenty years of the ascension, and Paul was in Greece by about AD 50. On his return to Jerusalem, Paul was taken by the Roman army to Caesarea, where he was imprisoned AD 57-9. His trial was transferred to Rome, which he reached early in AD 60, and where he stayed under house arrest. His death was probably in Nero's persecution of the Christians in AD 64 or shortly afterwards.

Paul's story begins in Tarsus, where he was born; but we first meet him in Jerusalem, which had not changed greatly since the years Jesus visited it.

We take up Paul's story again in Damascus, and follow his travels through present-day Syria, Turkey, Greece and Italy.

Tarsus

'I am a Jew,' said Paul to the officer commanding the Roman garrison in the Antonia fortress in Jerusalem, 'from Tarsus in Cilicia, a citizen of no mean city' (Acts 21:39).

Tarsus, Paul's birthplace, was the principal city of Cilicia, the most south-easterly part of Asia Minor. It stood in a fertile plain, on both banks of the river Cydnus, about ten miles from its mouth. The river was navigable as far upstream as Tarsus. Some thirty miles north of Tarsus were the Cilician Gates – the pass through the Taurus range which carried the main road from Syria into central Asia Minor. It is still a well-populated city, with about 40,000 inhabitants.

Tarsus was a city of great antiquity: it was a fortified trading centre before 2000 BC and is mentioned in Hittite records of the second millennium BC. It was destroyed in the invasions of the sea-peoples about 1200 BC, but some time later it was refounded by Greek settlers. For short periods in the ninth and seventh centuries BC it fell under Assyrian control. It enjoyed considerable autonomy under the Persian Empire, as capital of the satrapy of Cilicia; it was even permitted to issue its own coinage. In due course it passed into the hands of Alexander the Great. After his death in 323 BC it belonged to the dynasty of Seleucus I and his descendants, who succeeded to the eastern part of Alexander's empire. Under this dynasty it was called Antioch-on-Cydnus, but the name did not stick.

When Pompey established Roman dominance in that part of the world (67 BC), Tarsus became part of the Roman Empire, but retained its privileges as a free city. It was capital of the Roman province of Cilicia until 25 BC, but in that year Eastern Cilicia (in which Tarsus was situated) was detached from Western Cilicia and united with the province of Syria. It was Tarsus that witnessed the romantic first meeting of Antony and Cleopatra, described by Plutarch and embellished by Shakespeare.

In the later part of Antony's control of the Near East, Tarsus suffered under the maladministration of a nominee of his named Boethus. When Augustus overthrew Antony and became sole master of the Roman world, he entrusted the administration of Tarsus to one of its most illustrious sons, Athenodorus the Stoic, who had been Augustus's own tutor. Athenodorus reformed the city's constitution; it was probably he who fixed a property qualification of 500 drachmae for admission to the burgess roll.

Tarsus was a well-known centre of culture. Its schools taught the whole round of learning – philosophy and the liberal arts. In modern terms we might speak of the University of Tarsus though it was a civic university, catering for Tarsians, whereas Athens and Alexandria attracted many students from distant lands.

It was a prosperous city, renowned for some of its material products. Several authors refer to the linen which was manu-

A lorry emerging from the Cilician Gates. Carved on the illuminated rock to the left of the lorry is a Roman altar.

Flax, used chiefly for making linen, is the oldest textile fibre. The plants produce beautiful blue flowers whose seeds produce linseed oil.

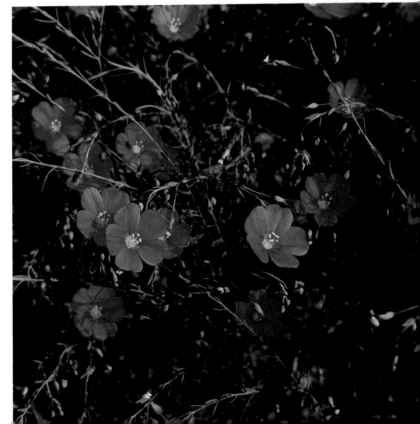

factured there from the flax which grew in the fertile plain around the city. We also hear of a cloth called *cilicium*, woven from goat's hair, which gave welcome protection against cold and wet. It may have been from this cloth that Paul learned to make tents. Perhaps he came of a tent-making family. His family appears to have been well-to-do, and over and above its economic prosperity it had received the rare honour of Roman citizenship. When Paul claimed to have been born a Roman citizen, this implied that his father had been a Roman citizen before him (Acts 22:28). How Roman citizenship came into the family we do not know. One archaeological scholar suggested that a firm of tent-makers could have proved very useful to the Roman army in those parts and received the citizenship as a reward, 'for services rendered'.

Although Paul was born in Tarsus, he may not have spent long there as a child. We may gather from Acts 22:3 that he grew up in Jerusalem. His parents were devout Jews, and probably judged that Jerusalem would be a more suitable environment for their son in his formative years than the pagan city of Tarsus. (Jerusalem, of course, merits inclusion among the places Paul knew, but the Jerusalem known to Paul was not much different from the Jerusalem described in Chapters 9 and 10.)

At a later date, however, after his conversion, Paul spent some years in and around Tarsus. After he had paid a short visit to

Falls on the River Cydnus, about one mile north of modern Tarsus.

The Taurus Mountains approached from the direction of Tarsus. Paul passed this way on his second and third missionary journeys.

Jerusalem in the third year after his conversion he was taken from there to Caesarea by some friends and put on board a ship bound for Tarsus (Acts 9:30). There, perhaps nine or ten years later, Barnabas found him and persuaded him to join him in Antioch and share the oversight of the Christian mission there (Acts 11:25, 26). We have no details of the years that Paul spent in and around Tarsus, but he was actively engaged in his apostolic ministry. It was during those years that news kept coming to the churches in Judea: 'Our former persecutor is now preaching the faith which he once tried to destroy' (Galatians 1:23).

Considerable excavation has been carried out in the Tarsus area, mainly on the mound called Gözlü Kule, where there was a western outpost of the Hellenistic and Roman city. (The adjective 'Hellenistic' refers to the Greek period from the conquests of Alexander the Great onwards.) The city's Roman theatre has been uncovered on Gözlü Kule, but the main buildings of the Roman period lie buried beneath modern Tarsus. Many buildings of Roman Tarsus are mentioned by contemporary writers, but only a few survive, and that in fragmentary form. These include the immense foundations of a temple, and a building decorated with mosaics which was discovered when foundations were being dug for a new courthouse in 1947. On the occasions when reconstruction is undertaken in the modern city, it is usually Byzantine remains that come to light.

Biblical references Acts 9:11

On the first occasion when Tarsus is mentioned in the New Testament, it is one of the indications given to Ananias of Damascus, who is being sent to speak to Paul, to help in identifying him. Ananias is told to go to such-and-such a street and knock at the door of a certain person's house, and ask for 'a man of Tarsus named Saul; for behold, he is praying'. Paul was part of the apostle's name as a Roman citizen, but as he was born into an observant Jewish family, belonging to the tribe of Benjamin (Romans 11:1; Philippians 3:5), his parents gave him a Jewish name – the name of the most illustrious member of the tribe of Benjamin in the history of Israel, King Saul. This was the name by which he was known in Jewish circles. Ananias would recognise him by three distinguishing features. The first two – his name and the name of his birthplace – are those which we should expect to be mentioned. The third – 'he is praying' – makes one think.

Damascus

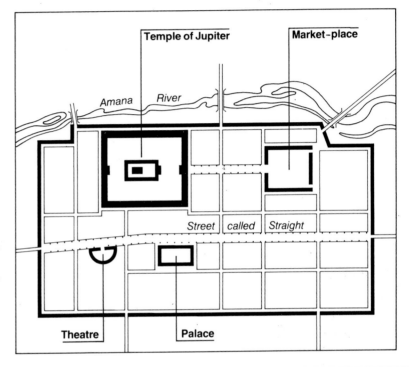

Looking down over modern Damascus, the ancient city where Paul intended to persecute Jesus' followers.

Damascus was a very ancient city by the time Paul journeyed there to arrest Christian refugees from Jerusalem. It occupied the same site as the Damascus of Old Testament times, but had changed beyond recognition. Since the eighth century BC it had been dominated in turn by the Assyrians, Babylonians and Persians, and then by Alexander the Great. After Alexander's death (323 BC) it was controlled first by the dynasty of the Ptolemies in Egypt and then (after 200 BC) by the rival dynasty of the Seleucids, whose capital city was Antioch.

When the Seleucid power collapsed, Damascus fell for a few years under the control of the kingdom of the Nabataean Arabs, which stretched from the vicinity of Damascus south to the Gulf of Aqaba, with its capital at Petra. But with the arrival of the Romans under Pompey in 64 BC, Damascus learned to live with a new and more durable master. It was included in the Roman province of Syria, but was linked in

a loose federation with a number of cities farther south – the Decapolis or 'league of ten cities'.

Not much of Roman Damascus is to be seen now. The east gate (Bab esh-Sharqi) may be of Roman date; it originally had three arches, but two of them have been walled up. In Hellenistic times Damascus was completely re-planned on the Hippodamian grid-system (so called after Hippodamus of Miletus, a town-planner of the fifth century BC). It had all the public installations which were regarded as essential to a Hellenistic city. When Herod the Great presented it with a gymnasium and a theatre, these were presumably designed to supersede earlier ones.

In Roman times Greek was the language most commonly heard in Damascus, but Aramaic would have been spoken there too, as it had been in the days of Ben-hadad and other Aramaean kings of whom we read in the Old Testament. Aramaic was the language of the Nabataean Arabs, who had a colony in Damascus administered by an ethnarch (mentioned in 2 Corinthians 11:32), and it would have been spoken by some members of the large Jewish community in the city.

Damascus figures in Muslim traditional belief as the place to which Jesus will descend at his second advent to destroy Antichrist (compare 2 Thessalonians 2:8). This belief may well go back beyond the Muslim conquest (AD 635), although it is not precisely documented before that.

In pre-Christian times there appears to have been a branch of the Qumran community in Damascus. This is inferred from a work called *The Book of the Covenant of Damascus*, discovered at the end of the nineteenth century in two incomplete manuscripts from the ancient synagogue of Old Cairo. This work tells of a body of pious Jews who 'went out from the land of Judah and sojourned in the land of Damascus', where they entered into a 'new covenant'. Not until the Qumran texts (the so-called Dead Sea Scrolls) came to light in 1947 and the following years was it realised that this body of pious Jews must have been associated with the Qumran community (the people of the Scrolls). It is not agreed by all that the 'Damascus' where they entered into a new covenant is to be understood literally and not figuratively, but most probably it is the literal Damascus that is meant. Those who made a covenant there believed that they were fulfilling Amos 5:27, which speaks of Jews going into exile beyond Damascus. These people's

The gateway to the traditional 'house of Ananias'.

exile was largely voluntary, because they disapproved so utterly of the regime which at that time held power in Judea. They had a clear idea in their own minds of how events would unfold at the time of the end, and one may wonder if they were the originators of the belief that Antichrist would meet his doom at Damascus.

One may wonder, too, if Paul had any contact with these 'covenanters' in Damascus after his conversion. His conversion took place as he was approaching Damascus with letters of extradition from the high priest in Jerusalem, authorising him to arrest and bring back in chains to Jerusalem followers of Jesus who had escaped from Jerusalem during the persecution that broke out after the stoning of Stephen. In one revolutionary flash he was confronted by the risen Christ. Against all his prejudices, he had no option now but to acknowledge the crucified Jesus as the risen Lord, who was there and then calling him

into his service. The law of Israel, which had hitherto occupied the central place in Paul's life, was instantaneously displaced by Christ. From that moment on, for him 'to live was Christ' (Philippians 1:21).

Temporarily blinded by 'the glory of that light' which he had seen (Acts 22:11), Paul had to be led by the hand into Damascus, and there he lodged for some days in the house of a man named Judas, in the 'street called Straight' (Acts 9:11). The present Darb al-Mustaqim ('Straight Street'), otherwise known as Suq et-Tawileh ('Long Bazaar'), probably follows the line of that ancient street.

There he was visited by Ananias, a Jewish resident of Damascus, 'a devout man according to the law' (Acts 22:12), who confessed Jesus as Lord. Ananias greeted Paul as a brother and welcomed him into the company of Christ's followers. Ananias seems not to have been one of the refugees from Jerusalem whom Paul had been sent to apprehend, although he knew all about the purpose of Paul's visit. There were apparently two groups of disciples of Jesus in Damascus – members of the Jewish community there and others who had fled from the persecution in Judea. These were the people with whom Paul first found Christian fellowship. It would be interesting to know if Ananias, or some of his fellow-disciples, had any connection with the 'covenanters of Damascus'; but we have no means of knowing.

Paul did not stay long in Damascus. He visited those synagogues to which he had been accredited as the high priest's ambassador, but he visited them now as the ambassador of another master. In those synagogues he proclaimed Jesus, saying, 'He is the Son of God' (Acts 9:20). But the risen Christ had called him specifically to be his messenger to the Gentiles (Galatians 1:16), so he left Damascus and spent some time among the Nabataean Arabs (Galatians

The 'street called Straight' was Paul's first refuge when blinded after his conversion. Here he was visited by Ananias.

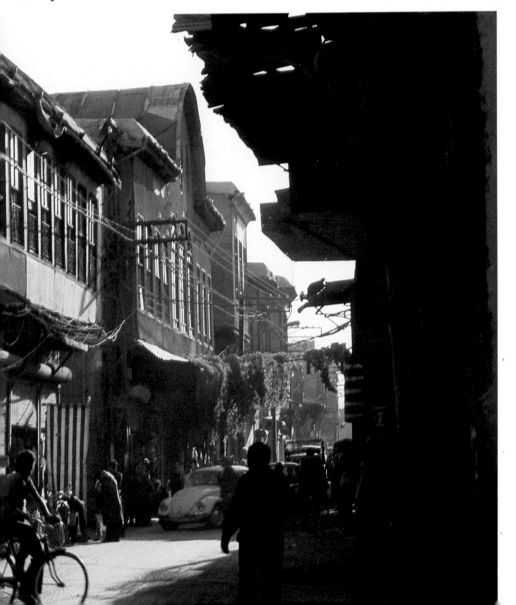

1:17). His activity among them was sufficiently provocative to attract the hostile attention of the Nabataean king, Aretas IV (9 BC–AD 40), for on his return to Damascus the local representative of Aretas guarded the city gate in the hope of arresting him. Paul was forced to make his escape in a basket let down through a window in the city wall (2 Corinthians 11:32, 33). It is believed by some historians that at this time Damascus formed part of the Nabataean kingdom, and it is pointed out that no Roman coins have been found at Damascus for the period AD 37-62. But this is by no means certain. Paul's escape from Damascus, at any rate, is the last occasion on which Damascus figures in the New Testament record.

'St Paul's Window' commemorates the apostle's nocturnal escape from arrest.

Biblical references Galatians 1:15-17; 2 Corinthians 11:32,33

There were two outstanding experiences associated with Damascus which Paul never forgot. One was unspeakably glorious: it was the revelation of Jesus Christ which he received or, as he puts it elsewhere, the occasion when he saw 'the light of the knowledge of the glory of God in the face of Christ' (2 Corinthians 4:6). The other was quite ridiculous: it was being let down in a basket through a window in the city wall to escape his enemies. But both taught him humility – the latter because, in his mind's eye, he must have cut such an absurd figure; the former because it brought home to him his total unworthiness to be granted such a revelation and to be called to serve the one who was revealed to him.

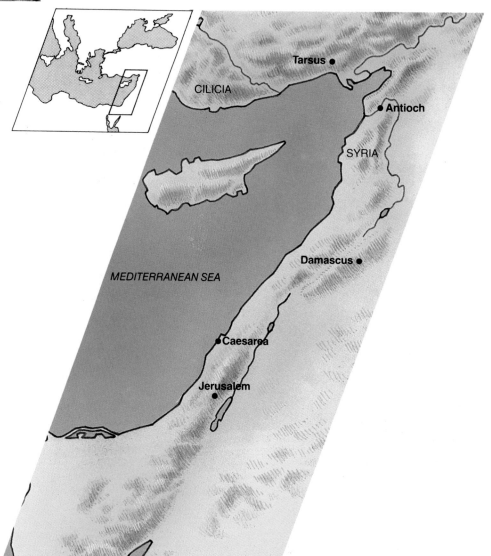

Antioch

There were sixteen cities called Antioch in the eastern Mediterranean world founded in the period after the death of Alexander the Great (323 BC). They owed their existence to rulers of the Seleucid dynasty which succeeded to the eastern part of Alexander's empire; many of the kings of that dynasty bore the name Antiochus, from which the place-name Antioch (*Antiocheia* in Greek) is derived. The greatest and best known of these cities is Antioch in North Syria,

Antioch-on-the-Orontes, founded by Seleucus I, first king of the Seleucid dynasty, in 300 BC and called after his father Antiochus. The city and the name survive to this day in Antakya, in the Hatay province of Turkey, which has a population of about 40,000.

Antioch, being a new city, was constructed on the most up-to-date town-planning principles, according to the Hippodamian grid-system. It was built

Antioch-on-the-Orontes was the third largest city in the Roman Empire in Paul's time. It was the centre of government of the province of Syria and Cilicia.

about sixteen miles upstream from the mouth of the river Orontes. At the mouth of the river stood its port, Seleucia Pieria (mentioned in Acts 13:4). The city walls of Antioch, the remains of which are still to be seen, ran along the hills overlooking the city and were extended seawards so as to enclose the port. (Similarly, the long walls of Athens in the fifth century BC were designed to protect the port of Piraeus and the approach to it.) Antioch originally stood on the south bank of the Orontes, but later kings extended it in various directions. One of them built a new ward of the city on an island in the river; in this island the royal palace was situated. Another king extended the city southwards to the foot of Mount Silpius, which runs parallel with the river. As a result of these extensions the city came to comprise four wards; each of these was separately fortified apart from the fortifications surrounding the whole city.

Antioch had a plentiful supply of better drinking water than the Orontes could supply, from the fresh springs at Daphne, five miles to the south. Here was a shrine dedicated to Artemis and Apollo. These were scarcely the Greek deities of those names; they were the Syrian goddess Astarte and her consort, newly equipped with Greek names. 'Daphnic morals' were a by-word in the Roman world for loose living. Antioch itself was sometimes distinguished from other cities of the same name by being called 'Antioch near Daphne'.

When Syria became a Roman province in 64 BC, Antioch became the seat of government of the imperial legate, who from 25 BC had charge of the united province of Syria and Cilicia. The city continued to be embellished with fine buildings: Herod the Great, for example, repaved its main east-west street with polished stone and adorned it with colonnades on both sides. The remains of this street and of another one, also colonnaded, can still be recognised. So can

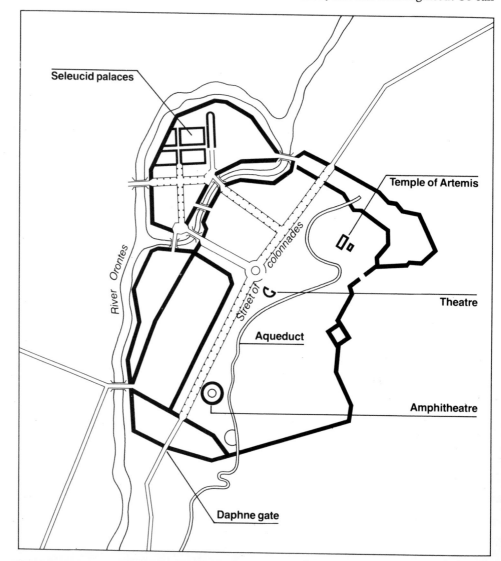

Seleucid palaces

River Orontes

Street of colonnades

Temple of Artemis

Theatre

Aqueduct

Amphitheatre

Daphne gate

the remains of the circus (north of the Orontes), palace (on the Orontes island), colonnaded forum, theatre, amphitheatre and public baths. An impressive wealth of mosaics from the floors of these and other buildings has come to light. In New Testament times Antioch ranked as the third largest city of the Roman Empire; it was surpassed only by Rome and Alexandria.

Antioch features in the New Testament as the first headquarters of Gentile Christianity. Even before Christianity reached the city, one Nicolaus, called 'a proselyte of Antioch', was one of the seven men appointed in the church of Jerusalem to supervise the daily distribution from the common fund (Acts 6:5). From its earliest days, there was a very large Jewish community in Antioch, and Nicolaus presumably belonged to it, though it would hardly have been in his native city that he became a Christian at that early date. But only a few years later it was at Antioch that the gospel was first presented to Gentiles on any significant scale.

As a result of the persecution of the church in Judea that was launched immediately after the death of Stephen, some Hellenistic disciples (i.e. those whose first language was Greek and who had affinities with the provinces north-west and south-west of Palestine) made their way north through Syria till they came to Antioch. Here some enterprising spirits among them – unnamed Jewish Christians from Cyprus and Cyrene – began to speak about Christ and his salvation to Gentiles whom they met. This was an innovation, but people were accustomed to innovations in Antioch. Here all sorts of nationality and religion met; here the Mediterranean world met the Syrian desert. People had their rough corners rubbed smooth, and traditional attitudes which were taken so seriously in a place like Jerusalem did not matter so much. Many Gentiles in Antioch, hearing the gospel for the first time, greeted it as the very message they were waiting for, and soon there was a flourishing church in Antioch, consisting mainly of Gentile believers. It was at Antioch that the followers of Jesus first came to be known as Christians; the name of Christ was so continually on their lips that they were recognised as his people.

When news of the innovation at Antioch came to the leaders of the mother-church in Jerusalem they did not panic but sent a suitable delegate to Antioch to see what was happening there and give such guidance as he thought fit. The man they chose was Barnabas, a Jewish Christian from Cyprus and a foundation member of the Jerusalem church. Barnabas was not the name his parents had given him; he received it from his fellow-Christians because it expressed his encouraging character (it means 'the son of encouragement'). Barnabas came to Antioch and was delighted by what he found there. He settled down among the Christians of the place and gave them all the encouragement they needed as they prosecuted their forward movement of evangelism among the Gentiles of the city.

The work developed and the church increased at such a pace in Antioch that Barnabas soon felt unable to cope with it single-handed, so he fetched his friend Paul from Tarsus to come to Antioch and share his ministry. Under their joint guidance the Christian cause in the city continued to flourish. Gentiles though the majority of the Christians of Antioch were, they did not forget their link with the mother-

A pass in the hills round Antioch, with a Byzantine gate from the old city walls.

The River Orontes at Antioch.

church. When they learned of an impending famine that was likely to hit Jerusalem with special severity, they sent Barnabas and Paul there with a gift which they had collected to enable their brothers and sisters to face the steep rise in the cost of food.

The Christians of Antioch recognised that the gospel, which had met the need of so many people in their own city, was bound to meet the need of other Gentiles farther afield. On one occasion, when the will of God was made known through a prophetic utterance in their church, they readily released Barnabas and Paul to undertake an extended campaign of evangelism in Cyprus and Asia Minor.

The Christian mission to Gentiles was attended by some practical problems. It took some time before Jewish Christians, with their ancestral food restrictions and other social customs, learned to mix freely with Gentile Christians. There was one awkward occasion when Peter, on a visit to

Antioch, felt obliged to desist from sharing meals with Gentile Christians because a message came to him telling of the embarrassment which his free-and-easy ways were causing to his fellow-disciples back home in Jerusalem. Not long after this the church of Antioch sent a delegation to Jerusalem to have these matters discussed and settled at the highest level. The result was a social accommodation (Acts 15:28, 29) which continued to be observed by Gentile Christians for a long time. As late as the closing part of the ninth century Alfred the Great incorporated it in his English law-code.

Antioch continued to be an important Christian centre for many centuries.

The 'Chalice of Antioch' is a silver cup set in a gilded open-work shell and mounted on a silver base, found in or near Antioch about 1910. It is now in the Metropolitan Museum of Art, New York. Some people liked to think at one time that the silver cup was the holy grail, the chalice used at the Last Supper; but its workmanship belongs to the fourth century AD.

Biblical references Acts 11:20-26
Christianity has for many centuries been reckoned to be a Gentile religion. Yet it originated as a movement within the Jewish nation. The Founder of Christianity and all his apostles were practising Jews. If we ask how it became detached from its Jewish matrix and acquired its predominantly non-Jewish character, we have to look to Antioch, the real birthplace of Gentile Christianity. The unnamed men of Cyprus and Cyrene who first thought of communicating the gospel to Gentiles in Antioch started something, the outcome of which they could never have foreseen.

Part of a Roman mosaic from Daphne, where fresh springs provided drinking water for Antioch. The splendour and wealth of Roman Antioch were reflected in buildings and rich mosaics.

The silver Chalice of Antioch, from the fourth century; evidence of continued Christian growth.

Galatia

The coastline of Asia Minor.

Galatia was a great Roman province in the heart of Asia Minor. It took its name from the Galatians, originally a group of Celts or Gauls that parted company with the main body of their fellow-tribesmen in Europe and moved south-east through the Balkan Peninsula, crossing into Asia Minor in the third century BC. There they settled in territory that had formerly belonged to the Phrygians. One of their principal cities, Ancyra, survives to the present day as the capital of Turkey, still bearing essentially the same name, Ankara.

The kings of Galatia became allies of the Romans, but when in 25 BC the last of those kings fell in battle against raiders from the Taurus mountain range, the Emperor Augustus took over his kingdom as a Roman province and incorporated in it a good deal of territory to the south, which the Galatian kings had never ruled.

We do not know if Paul ever visited that

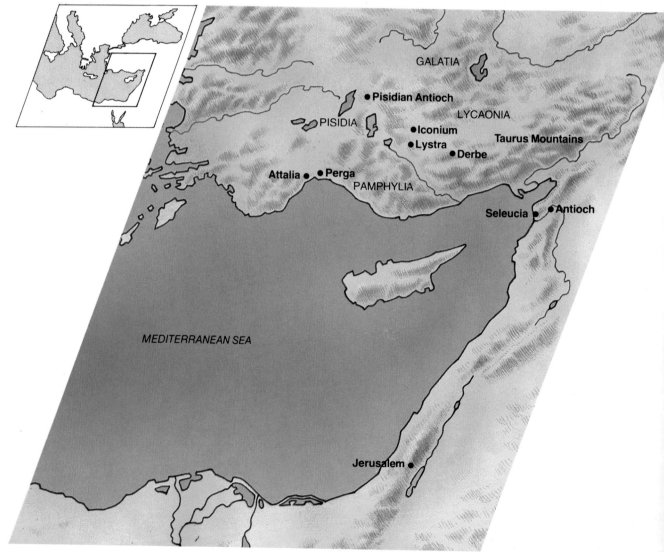

northern part of the province which had been the kingdom of Galatia. We do know of several cities in the southern part of the province which he visited. On the missionary tour, based in Antioch in Syria, which he undertook with Barnabas (Acts 13:4-14:26), he and Barnabas sailed from Paphos, the western capital of Cyprus, to the south coast of Asia Minor, and made their way to Perga, an important city of the Roman province of Pamphylia, lying six miles inland. From there they struck up country until they reached Pisidian Antioch. After preaching there they moved on in succession to Iconium, Lystra and Derbe; then they retraced their steps through the same cities, turning south again from Pisidian Antioch until they reached the port of Attalia from which they sailed back to the mouth of the Orontes and so returned to Antioch in Syria.

Two or three years later (perhaps in AD 49) Paul and Silas travelled from Antioch in Syria by land through the Cilician Gates into Central Asia Minor and visited Derbe and Lystra. From there they went on through 'the region of Phrygia and Galatia' (Acts 16:6) – that is, most probably, the region in which Iconium and Pisidian Antioch were situated. Three years later Paul made a hasty journey through the same area when on his way west to Ephesus he is said to have passed through 'the region of Galatia and Phrygia' (Acts 18:23).

There is good reason to believe that 'the churches of Galatia' addressed in Galatians 1:2 were the churches planted by Paul and Barnabas in Pisidian Antioch, Iconium, Lystra and Derbe. But whether that is so or not, these four cities were certainly places Paul knew.

Pisidian Antioch stood on a plateau about 3,600 feet high, two miles west of the modern Turkish town of Yalvaç. Sir William Ramsay suggested that Paul caught malaria in the low-lying area around

The port of Paphos, Cyprus, where Paul and Barnabas sailed for Asia Minor.

Sculpture from the temple near the Square of Augustus.

arches, connected it with the lower Square of Tiberius. To the east of the Square of Augustus stood a richly ornamented temple with Corinthian columns. The theatre lies in the western part of the city. Outside the city, on rising ground to the east, is the temple of Men Askainos, an important divinity in that part of Asia Minor.

The synagogue of Pisidian Antioch where Paul preached is not identified, but there were large Jewish colonies in the cities of Phrygia, both in Pisidian Antioch and in Iconium, the next city to which the two missionaries came.

Iconium lies nearly ninety miles east-south-east of Pisidian Antioch. The city and its name survive in modern Konya, the capital of the Turkish province of the same name. Then as now it was an important junction: the main east-west road from Syria to Ephesus passed through it. The Emperor Claudius bestowed his own name on it as an honorary prefix: Claudiconium.

Lystra, to which Paul and Barnabas moved from Iconium, was about eighteen miles south of that city. It was identified in 1885 with the mound of Zostera (near the town of Hatunsaray), when J.R.S. Sterrett found a Latin inscription there containing the name of Lystra. Like Pisidian Antioch, Lystra was made a Roman colony by Augustus.

In passing from Iconium to Lystra Paul and Barnabas crossed the regional frontier from Phrygia into Lycaonia. (A region was

Perga and came to this high ground to recuperate: he thought that malaria might be the 'bodily ailment' from which, as Paul says in Galatians 4:13, he was suffering when first he came to Galatia. This can be neither proved nor disproved.

Pisidian Antioch was founded as a border fortress soon after 300 BC. Augustus appreciated its strategic importance and made it a Roman colony in 6 BC. It became the military centre for the surrounding territory, and it was the starting-point for two roads built deep into the region of Pisidia to the south. Therefore, although it was not actually *in* Pisidia, it was known as Antioch near Pisidia, or Pisidian Antioch.

The site is now ruined, but the remains are still impressive. An aqueduct is particularly conspicuous; the city walls are also plainly to be seen. The main city square, the Square of Augustus, has been excavated; a monumental staircase and an entrance gateway (the propylaea) with three

The temple of Men Askainos, an important local divinity, stood outside Antioch.

The main street of Perga, six miles inland, on the way to Pisidian Antioch.

a subdivision of a province.) Over 400 years previously the Greek historian Xenophon referred to Iconium as 'the last city of Phrygia'. If Paul and Barnabas had well-tuned ears, they would realise soon after leaving Iconium that the indigenous population spoke a language which they had not heard before – 'the speech of Lycaonia' mentioned in Acts 14:11. When the people of Lystra planned to pay them divine honours, the missionaries' ignorance of this language meant that they did not grasp what was afoot until preparations for sacrificing to them were well advanced. Barnabas was identified with Zeus, the ruler of the gods, and Paul with Hermes, their messenger. There is evidence that these two divinities were worshipped conjointly in Lycaonia. In 1910 Sir William Calder discovered an inscription at Sedasa, south of Lystra, recording the dedication to Zeus of a statue of Hermes by men with Lycaonian names; sixteen years later he and W.H. Buckler discovered a stone altar near Lystra dedicated to the 'Hearer of Prayer' (presumably Zeus) and Hermes.

When Barnabas and Paul refused to accept worship from the people of Lystra, the people of Lystra soon turned against them: lending a ready ear to enemies of the missionaries who followed them from Iconium, they attacked them. Paul in particular was stoned, knocked unconscious and left for dead by the roadside (Acts 14:19). When, several years later, he drew up a catalogue of the hardships he had endured as an apostle, he says (referring to this occasion), 'Once I was stoned' (2 Corinthians 11:25). Nevertheless, he had reason to remember his visit to Lystra with gratitude: one of his converts there was Timothy, his future travelling companion and faithful helper.

Derbe has been identified as recently as 1957, when Michael Ballance found evidence pointing to Kerti Hüyük (a mound

Pisidian Antioch was a Roman military centre for the surrounding hill country. A starting-point for communications in Pisidia, the Roman colony had fine buildings, including a theatre.

about fifteen miles north-north-east of the city of Karaman) as the site. The evidence took the form of an inscription discovered on the mound, dedicated by the council and people of Derbe in AD 157 in honour of the Emperor Antoninus Pius. Derbe lay some sixty miles south-east of Lystra, so that the last words of Acts 14:20 should be translated, 'he set out with Barnabas for Derbe.' (They should not be translated in such a way as to suggest that Paul, after being knocked about so badly the day before, walked the 60 miles to Derbe in one day.)

It has been suggested that Paul and Barnabas went no farther than Derbe because there they reached the frontier of the province of Galatia. Across the frontier lay the territory of Antiochus, king of Commagene (AD 38-72), an ally of the Romans. Indeed, at times Derbe seems to have been governed by Antiochus; it was he who, in honour of the Emperor Claudius, named it Claudioderbe.

Hills above Iconium, modern Konya, which is on the main road from Ephesus to Syria.

Biblical references Galatians 3:1

'O foolish Galatians!' says Paul. In consequence, 'foolish' has sometimes come to be regarded as a 'permanent epithet' of 'Galatians', and commentators have made inept remarks about the natural fickleness and instability of the Celtic peoples (those commentators being themselves usually Anglo-Saxons or Germans). But there is no suggestion that Galatians were naturally foolish. What Paul means is that the particular Galatians to whom he was writing were foolish in one respect, and that a very important one. Having begun their Christian career through faith in Christ and the gift of the Spirit, they were behaving as though the new life, whose origin lay in the spiritual realm, could be brought to perfection through submission to external and bodily rites. Such a preposterous retrogression seemed to Paul a sign that his friends had taken leave of their senses.

Macedonia

Macedonia is a large territory in the Balkan Peninsula, by far the greatest part of which now forms the northern province of Greece, while other parts lie in Yugoslavia and Bulgaria. In antiquity it was a powerful kingdom. The Greek city-states of the classical period (fifth and fourth centuries BC) did not consider the Macedonians to be proper Greeks, although the Macedonian kings were keen patrons of Greek culture. One of the greatest of these kings, Philip II (356-336 BC), conquered the Greek city-states and founded a Graeco-Macedonian empire. Scarcely had he done so when he was assassinated, but his twenty-year-old son Alexander took up his father's heritage and in 334 BC led a united Graeco-Macedonian army into Asia. In a few years he had overthrown the Persian Empire. When he died in 323 BC his vast dominion did not long survive him as a united empire. Macedonia soon became a separate kingdom once more. From 221 BC relations between Macedonia and Rome were hostile, and after three wars Macedonia became a

Roman province in 146 BC.

Christianity reached Macedonia not more than twenty years after the death of Christ. Acts 16:9 tells of Paul's night-vision at Troas in which a man of Macedonia appeared to him, saying, 'Come over into Macedonia and help us.' Paul shared his experience with his three companions – Silas, Timothy and Luke – and they agreed with him that this was a call from God. They took ship from Troas, therefore, and in two days they landed at Neapolis, the modern Kavalla.

Neapolis was the eastern terminus of the Egnatian Way, the east-west Roman military road which ran across the Balkan Peninsula, from the Aegean Sea to the Adriatic. It was the most direct route between Rome and the east. A well-preserved Roman aqueduct, with three tiers of arches, is still to be seen at Neapolis; it carried water to the acropolis which defended the old city.

Apart from Neapolis, Luke mentions five Macedonian cities which Paul and his com-

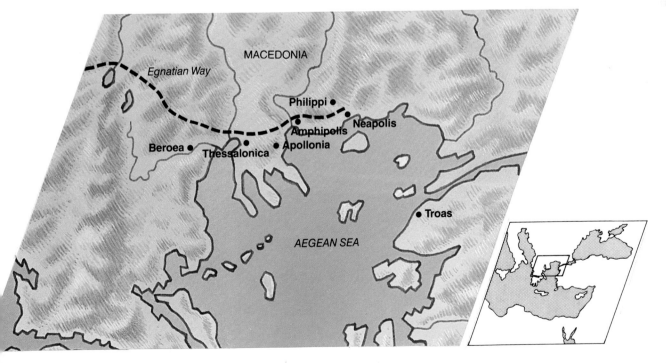

panions visited on this occasion: Philippi, Amphipolis, Apollonia, Thessalonica and Beroea. The first four of these stood on the Egnatian Way.

Philippi lay about thirteen miles inland from Neapolis, which served as its port. Philippi bore the name of its founder, Philip II of Macedonia; he established it in 356 BC on the site of an earlier settlement. Luke describes it in Acts 16:12 as 'a city of the first district of Macedonia' (the true reading is preserved only by a small min-ority of witnesses to the text). The 'first district' means the first of four districts into which the Romans divided Macedonia in 167 BC. Those familiar with Shakespeare's *Julius Caesar* remember how it was at Philippi that Caesar's assassins and their followers clashed in battle with his lieutenant, Antony and his adopted son, Octavian (later the Emperor Augustus). After the battle the victors, Antony and Octavian, re-constituted Philippi as a Roman colony and settled many of their veteran soldiers

The acropolis looks out over tiled roofs to the Aegean, over a church which shows Paul's message has not been forgotten.

there (42 BC). As a Roman colony, Philippi had a constitution modelled on that of the city of Rome: it was governed by two annually appointed chief magistrates (called praetors), whose police attendants were called lictors. The magistrates and police figure in the story of Acts 16:19-39.

There was evidently no Jewish community of any size in Philippi. In most cities which they visited, Paul and his companions made for the local synagogue, but there was none in Philippi: instead, they found an informal place of prayer outside the city on the west, by the river Gangites. Between the city and the river stand the remains of an arch, crossing the Egnatian Way, which may have been built to commemorate the city's receiving the status of a colony. The place of prayer probably lay to the west of this arch. Here a group of women met every sabbath day, and it was they who formed the nucleus of the church in Philippi. Their leader was Lydia, who traded in the purple dye for which her native city, Thyatira in

The evening departure of the fishing fleet from modern Kavalla harbour and their dawn return can hardly have changed in routine since Paul's day.

Fishing boats are built by hand in small shipyards by the sea.

The Roman aqueduct carried
water to the acropolis. Its three
tiers tower over a modern
house built into the lower arch.

Asia Minor, was renowned. A Latin inscription in Philippi mentions dealers in purple there. Two other women in the Philippian church, Euodia and Syntyche, receive honourable mention from Paul because of their co-operation with him in his gospel ministry (Philippians 4:2,3).

The site of ancient Philippi was excavated by French archaeologists between 1914 and 1938; more recently the work has been continued by the Greek archaeological service. The city stood both north and south of the Egnatian Way. The acropolis, over 1,000 feet high, on a spur of Mount Orbelos, overlooked the city from the north. At the foot of the hill are the remains of the large theatre, dating from the time of Philip II. On the south side of the Egnatian Way was the forum, some 300 by 100 feet. The forum buildings which can be seen today belong mostly to the age of Marcus Aurelius (AD 161-180), but they replaced others of an earlier period. It would have

been in the forum that Paul and Silas were dragged before the praetors. In the centre of the north side of the forum was a speaker's platform; at the north-west and north-east corners stood two large temples. On the west side were grain-shops, on the east side a library and reading room; on the south side was a colonnade, with a Roman agora to the south of it, while farther south still were a palaestra or gymnasium and Roman baths. There are also remains of Christian basilicas, but they belong to the Byzantine period; they present features similar to those of St. Sophia in Istanbul.

Thessalonica lies about 90 miles west of Philippi. Paul and his friends did not cover that whole journey in one day. Amphipolis and Apollonia are mentioned by name in Acts 17:1 because they were places where the missionaries stayed at least overnight on the Egnatian Way from Philippi to Thessalonica.

Thessalonica was founded about 315 BC

The port of ancient Neapolis was Paul's first landing in Europe, at the beginning of his journey west along the Egnatian Way to Philippi and Thessalonica.

Fishermen on the quay mending nets in the early morning.

The Roman forum where Paul and Silas were sentenced to imprisonment by the chief magistrates.

Looking down from the acropolis to the forum at Philippi. The Egnatian Way ran through Philippi roughly along the path of the modern road in the foreground. Philippi's acropolis dominated the Plain of Drama, with fine views of the surrounding mountains.

by the Macedonian king Cassander, who named it after his wife, a half-sister of Alexander the Great. When Macedonia became a Roman province, Thessalonica was the governor's headquarters, while it retained its municipal status as a free city, with its own magistrates, called 'politarchs' in Acts 17:6. This designation was peculiar to the magistrates of Macedonian cities; it appears on a number of inscriptions from the Roman period. The Egnatian Way ran through the city from east to west; part of the thoroughfare which follows its line bears the same name today.

Since it is still a large and populous city, Thessalonica does not lend itself so well to archaeological excavation. Some of the monuments which do survive from Roman times, like the Arch of Galerius which straddled the Egnatian Way near the east gate of the ancient city, and the neighbouring Rotunda (later St. George's Church), belong to a much later date than Paul's

lifetime – around AD 300. Until 1876 another arch, called the Vardar Gate, stood at the west end of the city: it bore an inscription (now in the British Museum) which mentioned the politarchs of Thessalonica.

Unlike Philippi, Thessalonica had a Jewish community with its synagogue, where Paul preached on the first three sabbath days after his arrival in the city. Here, among the fringe of God-fearing

A prison has been located among the excavations in Philippi. On the wall is a modern plaque, commemorating Paul and Silas's imprisonment: 'For me to live is Christ, to die is gain.' (Philippians 1:21).

The theatre was built into the foot of the acropolis.

The Egnatian Way ran from
Neapolis to Philippi, below the
acropolis.

Looking west, the road
winds through the valley
towards Thessalonica.

Gentiles who attended the services, Paul found the nucleus of his church, but the majority of his converts were pagans who, as he said, 'turned to God from idols, to serve a living and true God' (1 Thessalonians 1:9).

Paul had to leave Thessalonica because he and his companions were accused before the magistrates of disseminating subversive propaganda. He had perhaps intended to travel farther west along the Egnatian Way, but he was obliged to turn south for some fifty miles until he reached the city of Beroea (now pronounced Verria). Here he was given a more open-minded reception by the synagogue authorities than he had found in Thessalonica. We have few details about his converts in Beroea, except that they included several Greek women of high standing (Acts 17:12), and that one of his male converts was Sopater, who a few years later was one of a party accompanying him on his last journey to Jerusalem (Acts 20:4).

If (as is probable) he is identical with the Sosipater of Romans 16:21, he was evidently a Jew by birth, since Paul calls him 'my kinsman'.

Paul's first visit to Macedonia was punctuated by expulsions from one city after another. No wonder that when, a few weeks later, he arrived in Corinth, he could speak of coming 'in weakness and in much fear and trembling' (1 Corinthians 2:3). He possibly felt that his missionary work in Macedonia had been a failure. In fact it was an illustrious success. The Christianity which he planted in the cities of that province remains firmly rooted to the present day.

The Egnatian Way passed through villages by the lake. Paul rested at Apollonia, which was probably not very different from the modern village here.

Biblical references Philippians 3:20
'But our commonwealth is in heaven.'
James Moffatt translates this clause, 'But
we are a colony of heaven', and this translation links the text directly with the situ-
ation of the Christians in Philippi. Philippi
was a colony of Rome; it was, so to speak, a
small piece of Rome transplanted so as to
take root in a non-Roman environment, to
represent Rome and safeguard her interests.
Rome was their mother-city. So, says Paul,
a community of Christians (whether in
Philippi or anywhere else) is the city of God
in miniature, planted in this world not only
to maintain the interests of the mother-city
but also (unlike the citizens of Philippi) to
encourage the people around to join the
number of her free-born citizens.

After Paul's time the Roman
Arch of Galerius was built over
the Egnatian Way as it entered
Thessalonica from the east.
The modern main road follows
the same path, past the arch.

Houses in the backstreets of
Thessalonica, built on a steep
slope which rises behind the
town centre, within Byzantine
city walls.

Athens

Paul's brief visit to Athens, on his way from Macedonia to Corinth, is mentioned briefly by him in 1 Thessalonians 3:1 and described at greater length by Luke in Acts 17:15-34.

Athens has a continuous history of occupation as a Greek city from Mycenean times (before 1100 BC) to the present day. There was a short period during the Persian invasion under Xerxes in 480 BC when the Athenians had to leave their city and seek refuge on board their ships, but the invaders were soon defeated and the Athenians returned and rebuilt their ruined city. It remained a Greek city throughout the long centuries of Turkish rule.

Today it is the populous capital of Greece, but the heart of the city area is sufficiently cleared for the great monuments of its classical past to be conspicuously visible. Parts of a Mycenean defensive wall can be seen on the Acropolis, but most of the monuments date from the fifth century BC and later. Many of those that the visitor sees today were seen in a much better condition by Paul when he came to Athens in AD 50. Of all the buildings that crown the Acropolis the greatest is the Parthenon, the temple of Athene, the city's patron goddess. It was founded in 447 BC and even today is one of the most visually satisfying buildings to be seen anywhere in the world. In it stood the statue of Athene, the noblest work of the sculptor Pheidias. Some idea of the detail of the Parthenon can be appreci-

The acropolis of Athens and the Parthenon from the south-west. The acropolis commands a fine view of the sea and the port of Piraeus to the south. The Agora (market-place) lay north-west of the acropolis on the far side of the Areopagus, Mars Hill.

ated in the sculptures from its pediment now in the British Museum, among the so-called Elgin Marbles. During the Christian era the Parthenon was used successively as a church, a mosque and an arsenal; this last use was nearly its undoing when it was hit by a Venetian shell in 1687.

North of the Parthenon stands the temple of Erechtheus, with its six sculptured maidens or Caryatids fulfilling the function of columns for its southern portico; west of it stands the temple of Wingless Victory. The temple of Wingless Victory is built against the southern wing of the great gateway or Propylaea through which the Panathenaic procession made its way on to the Acropolis once every four years to present a new robe for the primitive wooden image of Athene housed in the temple of Erechtheus. The procession came along the Panathenaic Way from the north-west, through the Sacred Gate in the city wall.

At the foot of the Acropolis, built into its southern slope, is the Theatre of Dionysus, where the great dramas of classical Athens were staged. North-west of the Acropolis lies the Agora, the great Athenian marketplace, adorned with public buildings and colonnades. One of the colonnades, the Stoa of Attalus, has been restored and serves today as the Agora Museum. It was in the Agora that Paul entered into daily debate during his stay in Athens 'with those who chanced to be there', including philosophers

of the Epicurean and Stoic schools, both of which had their headquarters in Athens (Acts 17:17, 18).

Paul took everything in, but in his day the temples, altars and images were no mere antiquities or works of art, but installations of an active worship, false worship at that. 'His spirit was provoked within him as he saw that the city was full of idols' (Acts 17:16). One altar, however, attracted his special attention because of its unusual dedication: 'To an unknown god'. Other visitors to Athens about this time mention as a mark of the city's exceptional religiosity the 'anonymous altars' – altars to unknown gods – which it contained.

Why the altar spotted by Paul bore this particular inscription we cannot know. Perhaps, as has happened elsewhere, it was an old altar repaired by people who had no means of discovering the divinity to which it was originally dedicated, so they dedicated it 'to an unknown god'. But Paul saw how he could make use of this strange wording.

There was a venerable court in Athens which had jurisdiction in matters of religion and morals. Since Paul, with his talk of Jesus and the resurrection, seemed to be recommending a new religion, he was brought before it. It was called the Court of the Areopagus, because it met originally on the Areopagus, the hill of the war-god Ares, which rises on the west side of the Acropolis. By the first century AD, however, except on specially solemn occasions, the court is be-

Six maidens, caryatids, support the southern portico of the Erechtheion on the acropolis. The temple housed the shrine and olivewood statue of Athene.

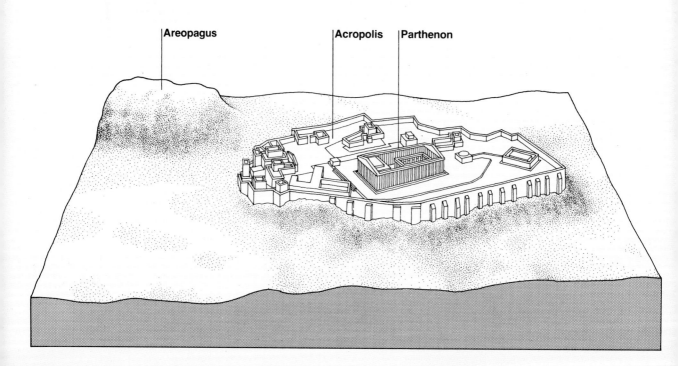

Areopagus | Acropolis | Parthenon

lieved to have met in the Royal Colonnade in the Agora, and it may have been there that it examined Paul. The statement that he was brought 'to the Areopagus' (Acts 17:19) may simply mean that he was brought before the court, and when he is described as 'standing in the middle of the Areopagus' (Acts 17:22) this probably means that he stood in the midst of the court, with its members sitting around him, rather than that he 'stood in the midst of Mars' hill', as the Authorised Version says. (How does one stand in the middle of a hill?)

No matter: when he was invited to expound his teaching, Paul referred to the Athenians as 'very religious' and recalled the altar inscription which had made such an impression on him. The 'unknown God' mentioned in the inscription was the very God whom he had come to make known, he said – the God who created all things and who, far from requiring anything from men and women, provided them with all that they needed. He supported his claims with quotations from Greek poets – 'In him we live and move and have our being' and 'we are indeed his offspring'. He then urged his hearers to have worthy thoughts of this God, who would call them to give an account one day to the man whom he had raised from the dead. Any who responded to Paul's preaching might well be said, like the pagans of Thessalonica, to have 'turned to God from idols, to serve a living and true God, and to wait for his Son from heaven, whom he raised from the dead, Jesus, who delivers us from the wrath to come' (1 Thessalonians 1:9, 10).

To most of Paul's hearers, this talk of a man being raised from the dead was absurd. He probably felt that he had achieved very little in Athens. A few converts are mentioned, but we find no reference to a church in Athens in Paul's day. Yet Athens was in due course to embrace wholeheartedly the message which he

The western face of the marble Parthenon, dedicated to Athene in 447 BC.

The Stoa of Attalus, a reconstruction of one of the two-tier colonnades in the Agora.

The lower floor of the stoa was a large, cool colonnade for meeting and discussion.

brought. The text of his address to the Areopagus is engraved on a bronze tablet at the foot of the ascent to the hill. A thoroughfare west of the hill is called 'Street of the Apostle Paul', and running off it towards the east, on the south side of the Acropolis, is the 'Street of Dionysius the Areopagite' (Paul's principal Athenian convert). Paul would be surprised, but no doubt gratified, could he know that his visit and preaching have been so well remembered.

Biblical references Acts 17:22-31
Paul's address to the Areopagus makes the following points:

The Doctrine of God
God is Creator of all.
God does not live in material buildings.
God needs nothing from human beings.
God supplies human beings with all that they need.
God is Judge of all.

The Doctrine of Man
The human race is one in origin and kinship.
The human race is the offspring of God.
The human race is designed to seek God and find him.
The human race should repent of its unworthy notions of God.
The human race is ultimately accountable to God.

The Man of God's Appointing
God has drawn near to men and women, and men and women may draw near to God, through the Man whom he raised from the dead, and through whom he is to 'judge the world in righteousness'.

Corinth

Corinth was an ancient city of Greece; its name, at least, goes back to pre-Greek times. It was situated on the Isthmus of Corinth (which was called after it) – the narrow neck of land which joins Central Greece to the Peloponnese, the peninsula which forms the southern part of mainland Greece. By its position it dominated the north-south land route, and it was equipped with two harbours. The western harbour, Lechaeon, on the Gulf of Corinth, com-municated with the central and western Mediterranean; the eastern harbour, Cenchreae (mentioned in Acts 18:18; Romans 16:1), communicated with the Aegean Sea and through it with the Black Sea and the eastern Mediterranean.

The ancient city was built on the north side of the hill called Acrocorinthus, which rises to a height of 1,900 feet and served it as a citadel. The citadel had an inexhaust-ible water supply in the upper spring of

The Doric Temple of Apollo was the only major Greek building to survive the Roman destruction and rebuilding of Corinth. The Acrocorinth towers behind the columns.

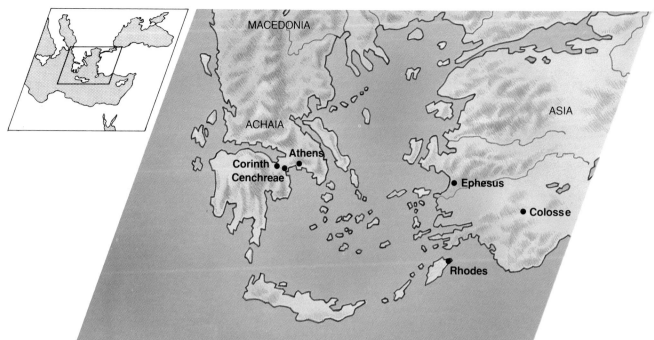

MACEDONIA

ACHAIA

ASIA

Corinth
Cenchreae

Athens

Ephesus

Colosse

Rhodes

The ruins of a Christian church in the harbour of Cenchreae, the eastern port of Corinth. Corinth also had a western port, Lechaeon, and was the centre of trade between Italy and Asia.

Peirene; a lower spring of the same name provided water for the city itself. Modern Corinth does not stand on the site of Old Corinth, but some three miles to the north; the site of Old Corinth therefore is completely accessible to archaeological exploration.

In classical Greek times Corinth attained great commercial prosperity; its name also became proverbial for licentiousness. It was a centre of the worship of Aphrodite, the goddess of love, whose temple stood on the summit of the Acrocorinthus. At the foot of the hill stood the temple of Melicertes, the patron of seafarers. The Isthmian Games, over which Corinth presided, and in which all Greek cities participated, were held every two years; at them the sea-god Poseidon was specially honoured. Corinth paid respect, as Paul put it, to 'many "gods" and many "lords"' (1 Corinthians 8:5).

Greek Corinth was utterly destroyed by a Roman army in 146 BC; this was its punish-

The Lechaeon road led from the gatehouse of Corinth to the western port.

Recent excavations have uncovered the stone starting line which indicates the site of a stadium for athletic games at Corinth. The slots in the stone acted as starting blocks for track events. The Isthmian Games were held between Corinth and Cenchreae probably while Paul was there. His familiarity with the games is evident from his letters.

ment for the leading part which it had played in a revolt against Rome. The only building of importance surviving from the period before that destruction is the Doric temple of Apollo, erected in the sixth century BC; seven great monolithic columns of this building still dominate the site. The city lay derelict for a century; then, in 44 BC, it was refounded as a Roman colony by Julius Caesar. Roman Corinth quickly regained the prosperity which Greek Corinth had enjoyed. The main roads and the two harbours were still at its disposal; in addition, a railroad of wooden logs, three and a half miles in length, was laid from west to east across the Isthmus so that ships might be dragged on it from the one harbour to the other. This railroad was called the *diolkos*.

Since Corinth was a Roman colony, all its citizens were Romans. It had many other residents, both Greeks and Jews, who were not citizens. One of Paul's earliest converts in Corinth, Gaius (1 Corinthians 1:14; Romans 16:23), was probably a Roman citizen; it is commonly believed that he is identical with the Titius Justus of Acts 18:7, and if so, then he bore an authentic threefold Roman name: Gaius Titius Justus.

When Paul first came to Corinth (in the autumn of AD 50), he visited the synagogue and was permitted, for a few weeks, to preach the gospel there, expounding the sabbath lessons from the Old Testament in such a way as to show that they pointed forward to Jesus. The museum of Old Corinth contains part of a stone lintel with a Greek inscription which, when entire, read 'Synagogue of the Hebrews'. If it did not stand over the doorway of the very synagogue where Paul preached (which is not impossible), it belonged to a building which replaced the synagogue of Paul's day.

Another inscription, found in Corinth by American archaeologists in 1929, was engraved on a marble slab; it informs us in Latin that 'Erastus, in commemoration of his aedileship (curatorship of public buildings), laid this pavement at his own expense'. The inscription seems to belong to the first century AD and refers, in all probability, to that Erastus who is mentioned in Romans 16:23 as 'city treasurer' of Corinth. If this is so, then we should gather that Erastus performed his duties as aedile so well that he was promoted to a higher and more responsible office.

When Paul in 1 Corinthians 10:25 refers to people in Corinth buying meat in the 'meat market', he uses the Greek word *makellon*. This word has been found in another Corinthian inscription which indicates that the meat market was situated somewhere along the paved Lechaeon Road. Many shops and colonnades have been uncovered by archaeologists around the fine square Roman agora (market-place). In the centre of the agora is an impressive stone platform which figures in the New Testament narrative. This is the 'tribunal' from which Gallio pronounced judgment

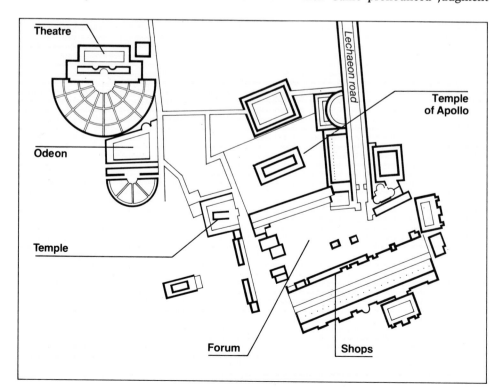

when Paul was accused before him of propagating an illegal religion (Acts 18:12-17). Corinth, in addition to being a Roman colony, was the seat of administration of the Roman province of Achaia. When Gallio was sent from Rome to be proconsul of Achaia in AD 51, it was in Corinth that he took up residence. He refused to take up the case against Paul, because he concluded that the dispute was over rival interpretations of the Jewish law. But his judgement, though negative, was in effect a favourable one so far as Paul was concerned; it confirmed his liberty to carry on with his apostolic work. An adverse judgement would have been a great handicap to him, for Gallio was an important and influential person, whose verdict would be followed as a precedent by many Roman magistrates throughout the empire.

Biblical references 1 Corinthians 2:1-5; Acts 18:9,10

Paul arrived at Corinth in a mood of dejection and apprehension. He had practically been driven out of Macedonia, and his reception in Athens had been lukewarm. Corinth had probably not figured on his original itinerary, and the reputation of the city was such that he could scarcely expect the gospel to make much of an impact there. He was greatly in need of the heavenly encouragement which came to him in a night vision shortly after his arrival in Corinth. But he stayed in Corinth for eighteen months, and when he moved on at the end of that period, he left behind him a large and gifted, if volatile, church. It is plain from his two letters to the Corinthians that the church which he planted there caused him many a headache: it was turbulent and unruly, but it was undoubtedly alive, and remains so to this day.

Corinth

The Roman public baths at Corinth, with private cubicles under the arches.

Ephesus

The view of Mount Pion from Mount Coressus, with the odeon (small theatre) built into its slopes. The centre of Ephesus was on the plain at the foot of Mount Pion, below the odeon and town hall.

Ephesus stood at the mouth of the river Caÿster, which flows into the Aegean Sea. In the days before the Greeks (more precisely, the Ionians) colonised that part of western Asia Minor, there was a settlement of Carians on the site. These Carians worshipped the great mother-goddess of Asia Minor and probably called her Artemis – the name is non-Greek. When the Ionian colonists arrived, they intermarried with the Carians and joined in the worship of their goddess. Artemis first appears in art and literature as the guardian of wild-life. Her temple at Ephesus housed her image, which was believed to have 'fallen from the sky' (Acts 19:35). An earlier temple than that which stood there in New Testament times was burned down in 356 BC – on the

very night, people said, when Alexander the Great was born. The young man who set fire to it said that he had done so in order that his name might go down in history. He achieved his aim, for if we know nothing else about him, we know his name – it was Herostratus.

The magnificent temple which replaced the one burnt by Herostratus was one of the seven wonders of the ancient world. It covered an area four times as extensive as the Parthenon in Athens; it was supported by 127 columns, each of them sixty feet high, and it was adorned by some of the greatest sculptors of the age. But it disappeared completely; for centuries no one knew where it had stood, until its site was identified beyond all doubt on the last day of 1869 by J. T. Wood. Its foundations were then discovered in a marsh at the foot of the hill of Ayasoluk, near the town known today as Selçuk. On the hill of Ayasoluk stand the remains of a later shrine – the basilica of St. John the Divine, erected by the Emperor Justinian (AD 527-565). Its high altar covers the traditional tomb of John. The very name Ayasoluk preserves the apostle's memory: it is a corruption of the Greek phrase meaning the 'holy divine'.

Roman Ephesus, the city that Paul knew, stood about one and a half miles south or south west of the temple of Artemis. Its site is an archaeologist's paradise, for it is unencumbered by any modern settlement. The whole area has for many years been excavated systematically by Austrian archaeologists, and as successive streets and buildings are uncovered and restored, they

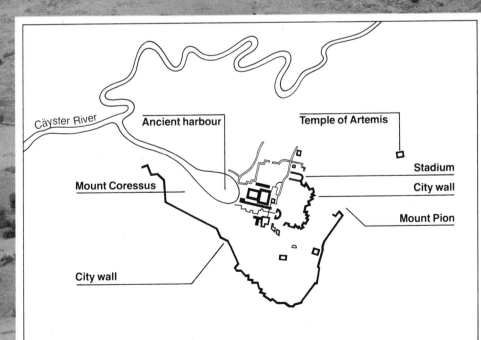

Statue of 'Great Artemis of the Ephesians', worshipped when Paul visited Ephesus.

The Temple site seen from the Basilica of St John the Divine on the Hill of Ayasoluk.

The Hill of Ayasoluk from the lower entrance to Roman Ephesus. The Temple of Artemis, once one of the seven wonders of the world, stood at the foot of the hill.

make a magnificent impression.

In New Testament times Ephesus was a seaport; the harbour had to be dredged continuously to clear it of the silt washed down by the river Caÿster. As the city decayed, the harbour was neglected, and today Ephesus stands seven miles inland. As one looks west from the topmost tiers of the theatre it is possible to discern the outline of the ancient harbour, almost as in aerial photography; it is now a marshy waste at the end of the paved street called the Arcadian Way. To the right of the Arcadian Way, as one looks down from the theatre, stand the twin churches of St. Mary, in which the Council of Ephesus was held in AD 431. The theatre itself, a vast open-air auditorium built into the western slope of Mount Pion, could seat 24,000 people. The civic assembly regularly met in the theatre on appointed dates. The theatre was also the venue for the very irregular assembly which Luke describes in Acts 19:29-41, when the populace staged a two-hour demonstration in honour of 'Great Artemis of the Ephesians' and in opposition to Paul and his associates.

There is no evidence that Paul spoke disparagingly in public about the great goddess: in fact, the town clerk of Ephesus, in the speech which he made to quieten the demonstrators in the theatre, absolved him and his associates of any such offence. But every one knew that he did not believe in her, and when he made converts among the pagans of Ephesus, they abandoned her worship. This naturally caused concern to those whose livelihood depended on her worship, like the guild of silversmiths, who manufactured religious souvenirs and amulets, and miniature replicas of the goddess in her shrine. Silver reproductions of her image and terracotta models of her temple have been found. An inscription of AD 104, half a century after Paul's visit, tells how a Roman official presented a silver

Looking down towards the site of the harbour at the end of the Arcadian Way. The theatre in the foreground was the venue for the Ephesians' demonstration against Paul.

A coin of Ephesus from Roman times, depicting Artemis the many-breasted goddess in her famous temple.

The Arcadian Way led from the theatre to the ancient port. The coastline is now six miles away as the river has silted up over the centuries.

image of Artemis, together with other statues, to be set up in the theatre during a meeting of the civic assembly.

Demetrius, president of the guild of silversmiths, had reason to be concerned at the threat to his trade. But his concern was not purely economic: he is described in terms which suggest that he was one of the twelve members of the 'vestry' of the temple of Artemis. And what he feared came to pass – not immediately, but in the course of a few centuries: the advance of the gospel inevitably meant the diminishing of the worship of Artemis, until at last she was 'deposed from her magnificence' (Acts 19:27). Then, centuries later, people of yet another faith took possession of the country, and the churches of St. Mary and St. John fell into ruins in their turn. But the record of Paul's ministry in Ephesus, and the two letters to the Ephesians in the New Testament – one by Paul, the other from the risen Lord through his servant John (Revelation 2:1-7) – remain as a powerful proclamation of the Christian gospel.

We do not know where Paul lived in Ephesus. The Jewish synagogue in which he preached during the first few weeks of his stay has not been located yet, nor is there any means of identifying the school of Tyrannus, where for two years he lectured around midday, when Tyrannus and his pupils were taking their siesta. We know that Paul was exposed to repeated dangers during his Ephesian ministry. On an eminence to the south of the former harbour stands a ruin which is called 'St. Paul's Prison'. It has no historical title to be so called, but the tradition that Paul was imprisoned for a period while he was in Ephesus may be well founded.

Near the Magnesian Gate, south-east of Mount Pion, an early Christian shrine has been identified in a cave, with graffiti invoking Paul. But in Christian tradition the great name associated with Ephesus is that of John. Not only so, but in view of the statement in John 19:27 that the beloved disciple took the mother of Jesus to his own home after the crucifixion, it came to be believed that when he migrated to Ephesus she accompanied him. One testimony to this belief is presented by the twin churches of St. Mary already mentioned; another, overlooking the site of Ephesus, is a building venerated since 1891 as the house of the Virgin Mary; it has received no official recognition, but has twice in recent years been honoured by a papal visit.

Biblical references 1 Corinthians 16:8,9
Towards the end of his long missionary stay in Ephesus, Paul wrote to his friends in Corinth, promising to pay them a visit soon, but, he added, 'I will stay in Ephesus until Pentecost, for a wide door for effective work has opened to me, and there are many adversaries'. He was writing probably about Easter (in AD 55), and he had been in Ephesus for two and a half years. Great opportunities and great opposition were to Paul familiar experiences in his apostolic work, and each was usually accompanied by the other. By this stage in his career Paul had learned how to turn opposition into opportunity, and so thoroughly did he prosecute his ministry in Ephesus that Christianity persisted in that part of Asia Minor for centuries after the Turkish conquest, and disappeared only with the wholesale exchange of Greek and Turkish populations which followed the Graeco-Turkish war of 1923.

Caesarea

Caesarea Maritima – Caesarea-on-Sea, as we might say – was built by Herod the Great between 22 and 9 BC to serve as an adequate seaport on the Mediterranean coast of Judea. There was an earlier settlement there, with a fortification called Straton's Tower, called after a Sidonian ruler who flourished about 330 BC. We know that a harbour of sorts had been constructed there by 259 BC, for it is mentioned in one of the Zenon papyri, a collection of documents from an Egyptian finance officer (at that time Palestine belonged to the kingdom of the Egyptian Ptolemies).

Excavations at Caesarea since 1959 have revealed something of the magnificent scale of Herod's buildings, but most impressive of all was the great artificial harbour, enclosed by two massive stone breakwaters. These were examined in 1960 by the Link Mission for Underwater Exploration, and it was established that they enclosed a semicircular area of about three and a half acres.

Josephus describes the huge blocks of stone which were let down into twenty fathoms of water to serve as foundations for the breakwaters. The entry to the harbour was from the north-west. The harbour installations were on a scale appropriate to such an engineering masterpiece. An earthquake in AD 130 caused considerable damage to the structures.

Two parallel aqueducts conveyed water to Caesarea – one of Herod's period, bringing water from springs on the southern slope of Carmel, and a later one bringing a further supply from the Crocodile River, about six miles north of Caesarea.

Herod called the city Caesarea, after his patron Caesar Augustus. A fine temple in the emperor's honour, probably dedicated to 'Rome and Augustus', was erected on an artificial mound of stone, fifty feet high, facing the harbour. The royal palace also stood on this mound. The vaulted chambers which supported the mound are still to

The mosaic floor of a Byzantine Christian building where a statue of the Good Shepherd was found.

be seen.

In the southern part of the city Herod built a theatre facing the sea. This was excavated about 1960 by Italian archaeologists. Its acoustic properties can readily be tested; they bear witness to the skill with which it was constructed. One stone found there contains part of a Latin inscription in which Pontius Pilate, 'prefect of Judea' (AD 26-36), is said to have dedicated a public building in honour of the Emperor Tiberius (AD 14-37). During a later reconstruction of the theatre the stone was built into the steps; the reconstructors did not realise how important the inscription would be for future archaeologists.

Farther east than the theatre, Herod built a hippodrome, while to the north of the city there was an amphitheatre, used for athletic sports and for gladiatorial and wild beast shows.

The history of Caesarea continues into Byzantine and Crusader times. Among Byzantine buildings are successive synagogues of the fourth and fifth century (probably on the site where the Herodian synagogue stood) and a Christian building

(apparently not a church) which contained a statue of the good shepherd and a mosaic showing a quotation from Romans 13:3.

Caesarea in New Testament times was a predominantly Gentile city, though it had a considerable Jewish population. When Judea became a Roman province in AD 6 and was administered by a succession of governors appointed by the emperor, the governors took up residence in Caesarea. When public order required their presence in Jerusalem, as at the great pilgrimage-festivals, they moved there; but normally they felt more at home in Caesarea. There the royal palace that Herod had built for himself served as their residence. In Acts 23:35 it is called 'Herod's praetorium'

The beach at Caesarea, once enclosed by massive breakwaters, forming an artificial harbour.

(praetorium being a technical term for the commander-in-chief's headquarters). The governors of Judea who figure in the New Testament – Pilate, Felix, Festus – all resided here. As the governors were supreme commanders of the Roman military forces in the province, detachments of Roman troops were regularly stationed in Caesarea.

When Paul paid a brief visit to Jerusalem in the third year after his conversion to make the acquaintance of two leaders of the mother-church, Peter and James, his presence in the city became known to his enemies. His new friends therefore judged that it would be best for his safety – and no doubt for theirs – if he left Jerusalem as soon as possible, so some of them escorted him to Caesarea and put him on board a ship bound for his native Tarsus. As they watched its sails disappear over the horizon, they probably breathed a sigh of relief. 'Then the church had peace,' says Luke (Acts 9:31).

Paul was not the only apostle to visit Caesarea; Peter went there on at least one occasion, when he was sent to preach the gospel to the Roman centurion Cornelius, a non-commissioned officer of the Augustan cohort (Acts 10:1-48).

It was in Caesarea that Herod Agrippa the elder (grandson of the city's founder) was making a public oration at a festival in honour of the Emperor Claudius when he was suddenly attacked by severe internal pains which ended only with his death five days later (AD 44). The incident is recorded by Luke (Acts 12:21-23) and, in rather greater detail, by Josephus.

When Paul completed his last voyage from Greece to Palestine, together with a

A Roman wheat ship from North Africa, pictured on a coin of the Emperor Commodus.

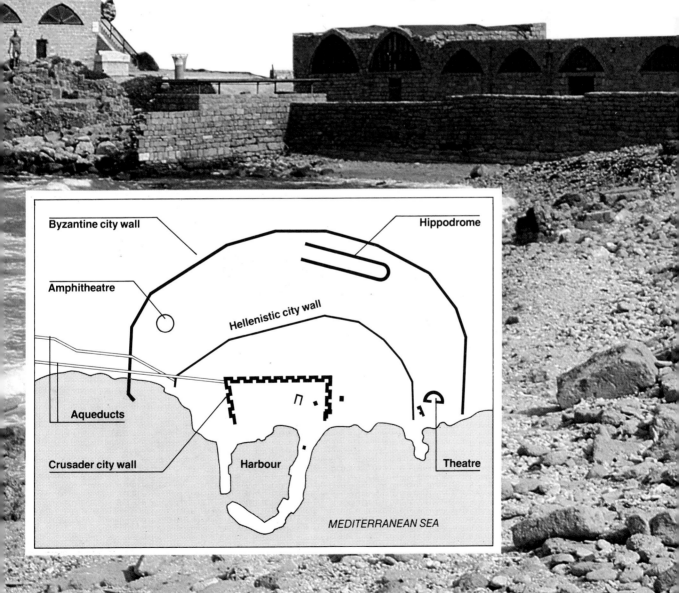

Byzantine city wall

Hippodrome

Amphitheatre

Hellenistic city wall

Aqueducts

Crusader city wall

Harbour

Theatre

MEDITERRANEAN SEA

number of companions from his Gentile mission-field (Luke among them), he arrived at Caesarea and there the party spent several days in the house of Philip the evangelist. Twenty years previously Philip, after his mission in Samaria and his fruitful meeting on the Gaza road with the royal treasurer from Ethiopia, travelled north along the Mediterranean coastal road, evangelising each place to which he came, until he arrived in Caesarea (Acts 8:4-40). There he appears to have settled down and raised a family; when Paul and his companions visited him they were impressed by Philip's four daughters, each one a prophetess. Many years later, when these daughters were old ladies, they lived at Hierapolis in Phrygia and were much sought after as informants about persons and events in the early church.

Paul and his friends then left Caesarea for Jerusalem, but in less than two weeks Paul was back in Caesarea, through no choice of his own. He was taken into protective custody by the Roman army in Jerusalem, to save him from being beaten to death by a hostile mob in the temple precincts, and when the commanding officer in the Antonia fortress discovered that he was a Roman citizen, he decided to send him for safety to Caesarea. To Caesarea, then, he sent him under armed guard to Felix (Roman governor of Judea from AD 52 to 59). There Paul was kept in Herod's praetorium for two years, until Felix was replaced as governor by Festus. Then, fearing that Festus' inexperience might expose him to his enemies in Jerusalem all over again, Paul exercised his privilege as a Roman citizen and appealed to have his case transferred to the tribunal of the emperor in Rome. It was at Caesarea, on the eve of his being sent to Rome, that Paul had the opportunity of giving an account of his conversion and ministry before Herod Agrippa the younger (son of that Herod

An inscription recording Pontius Pilate's dedication of a building in honour of Tiberius Caesar.

Agrippa who had met a sudden death in Caesarea fifteen years before).

During Paul's imprisonment in Caesarea (AD 57-59), tension between the Gentile and Jewish populations of the city increased to the point where outbreaks of violence took place between the two communities. The ineptitude with which this trouble was handled by the provincial administration and even by the authorities in Rome played its part in fostering the anti-Roman feeling among the Jews of Judea which came to a head in the revolt of AD 66.

Biblical references Acts 9:30; 23:23-33
On two occasions, the one very early in his Christian career, and the other more than twenty years later, Paul had to be taken for safety's sake from Jerusalem to Caesarea. He speaks in 2 Corinthians 11:26 of being in 'danger from my own people' and 'danger from Gentiles', but the danger which he encountered from time to time in Jerusalem seems to have been specially acute, so that he, 'a Hebrew born of Hebrews' (Philippians 3:5), found greater relative security in a mainly Gentile city. Why should this be?

The Roman aqueduct which once supplied Caesarea with freshwater from the north.

The reconstruction of Herod's theatre, built facing the Mediterranean Sea.

Rome

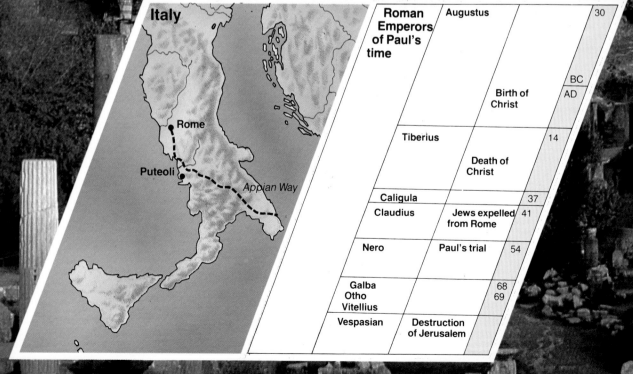

Italy

Rome

Puteoli

Appian Way

Roman Emperors of Paul's time			
Augustus			30
			BC
	Birth of Christ		AD
Tiberius			14
	Death of Christ		
Caligula			37
Claudius	Jews expelled from Rome		41
Nero	Paul's trial		54
Galba Otho Vitellius			68 69
Vespasian	Destruction of Jerusalem		

In Paul's day Rome was the greatest city in the world, dominating the whole Mediterranean area, with all Europe west of the Rhine and south of the Danube, and all south-western Asia west of the Euphrates.

It is difficult for us, in this day of great super-powers, to realise how a single city could create for itself a power-base from which it could control a great part of the known world. Yet history knows of many such cities, and Rome is the best known of all.

Rome originated as a group of pastoral hill-settlements in the plain of Latium in Italy, on the left bank of the Tiber, about fifteen miles upstream from the mouth of the river. These settlements combined to form a city, which by stages dominated the

Looking south-east from the Capitoline Hill over the Roman Forum. The Via Sacra runs from the lower left towards the Arch of Titus. Both the arch and the Colosseum on the skyline post-date Paul, but show the magnificence of the capital city of the Roman Empire he knew.

plain of Latium, then the greater part of Italy, then Sicily and Sardinia, and so, after conquering the rival city of Carthage in modern Tunisia, to the mastery of the Mediterranean world.

As this empire extended, citizenship of Rome was not confined to freeborn natives of the capital: it was conferred, judiciously, on people in the provinces who had served Roman interests in some outstanding way, and once a man received Roman citizenship, all his descendants inherited the honour. Paul, a native of the province of Cilicia, was born a Roman citizen (Acts 22:28), which means that his father must have been one before him.

It was only after many years of apostolic activity in the eastern provinces of the Roman Empire that Paul at last had the opportunity of visiting the city of which he was a citizen by birth. He had set out for it more than once before, but had always been sidetracked. When he first came to

Philippi and Thessalonica, he found himself on the Egnatian Way, which ran west to the Adriatic coast, from which there was a short sea-crossing to Brindisi in Italy, and from there the Appian Way led to Rome. Perhaps even then he had some idea of following this route, but he was prevented from doing so, and turned south instead of proceeding west. Nearly ten years later he achieved his ambition of seeing Rome, but in a way which he could not have foreseen. He came to Rome as a prisoner, under military guard, to stand his trial before the emperor, to whose jurisdiction he had appealed from the provincial court in Judea.

By the time Paul reached Rome (early in AD 60) there were many Christians there. Three years previously Paul had written a letter to the Christians in Rome (preserved in our New Testament as the Letter to the Romans) to prepare them for his projected visit – which at that time he hoped to pay as a free agent. When at last he was being

The worn paving stones of the Appian Way, the main route Paul followed to Rome.

The pyramid of Gaius Cestius on the Ostian Way, which Paul would have seen in his day.

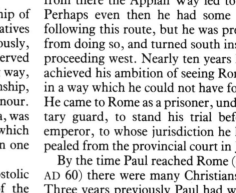

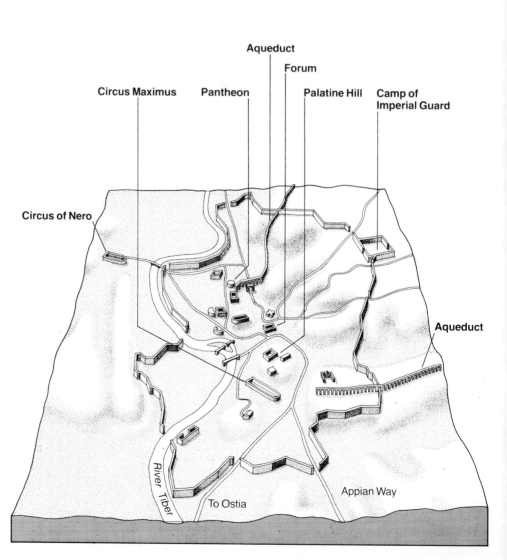

Aqueduct

Forum

Circus Maximus   Pantheon   Palatine Hill   Camp of Imperial Guard

Circus of Nero

Aqueduct

River Tiber

To Ostia

Appian Way

taken to the city along the final stages of the Appian Way, some Roman Christians walked out along the road for thirty or forty miles to greet him and escort him for the remainder of his journey. The sight of these friends brought Paul much encouragement.

It is impossible to be sure when Christianity was first brought to Rome. Priscilla and Aquila, who were among the Jews expelled from Rome by the Emperor Claudius in AD 49, met Paul in Corinth next year and became his firm and lifelong friends. Yet he never speaks of them as though they were converts of his, and the probability is that they were members of the primitive Christian community in Rome before they were forced to leave the city.

Having arrived in Rome, then, Paul spent the next two years there, 'in his own hired house', as the AV says – not an exact translation, perhaps, but one that spells out what is really meant by the RSV 'at his own

St Pauls Outside the Walls, the great basilica over the traditional site of Paul's tomb.

The gardens of the Abbey of Three Fountains, three miles from Rome, on the Ostian Way. The abbey marks the traditional site of Paul's execution during Nero's persecution of the Christians.

expense'. *Where* he stayed in Rome we can only guess – possibly on the third floor of a tenement, where the rent would be cheaper. He was not free to come and go as he chose, because he was constantly handcuffed to a soldier. The soldier was relieved by a comrade every few hours, but there was no such relief for Paul.

Visitors to Rome are shown the Mamertine prison, north-west of the Roman forum, as the place where both Paul and Peter spent their last days in the condemned cell. If there is any truth in this tradition, so far as Paul is concerned, it must refer to a later phase than the two years of Acts 28:30. That Paul was ultimately condemned to death and led out for execution by the third milestone along the Ostian Way is reasonably certain, although there is no record of this in the New Testament. The traditional site of his execution by the sword may be seen today in

Terracotta houses in central Rome reflect the setting sun. Below their windows are the imperial fora of Trajan and Augustus, across the way from the Roman Forum.

the monastic enclosure of Tre Fontane; the great basilica of St. Paul Outside the Walls covers the traditional site of his tomb. The present basilica, completed in 1854, replaces a magnificent fourth-century structure, which was accidentally burned down in 1823. In the first century the area was a public burial-ground; so, incidentally, was the area covered by St. Peter's in Vatican City, where the apostle Peter is (with good reason) believed to have been buried.

As today we view the monuments of imperial Rome, we have to remind ourselves that some of the most familiar of them were not there in the apostles' time. The Roman Forum was there, and the Sacred Way ran through it, but there was no Arch of Titus at the east end nor Arch of Septimus Severus at the west end. The best-known of Roman monuments, the Colosseum, was begun ten or twelve years after Paul's death.

On the other hand, Paul saw much that cannot be seen today. He saw the city as it had been restored by the Emperor Augustus (27 BC – AD 14), who boasted that he had 'found a city of brick and left a city of marble'. Just over four years after Paul's arrival, the great fire of Rome broke out (in July, AD 64) and destroyed a good part of the city. As is well known, the fire was followed by Nero's victimisation of the Christians of Rome. Tradition assures us that Peter and Paul were the most distinguished victims of this persecution, but it certainly claimed as martyrs a great number of ordinary Christians who have left no name.

As Paul first approached Rome by the Appian Way, he saw by the roadside some monuments which survive, if only in a ruined condition, to our own day – the tomb of Cecilia Metella, for example, and, nearer the city, the tomb of the Scipios. As

Looking across the River Tiber over Rome from the dome of St Peter's

he was led out of the city along the Ostian Way he would have seen the pyramid of Gaius Cestius (but the wall of Aurelian, into which it is now built, is 200 years later than Paul's time).

There was a large Jewish population in Rome in Paul's time; almost as many Jews lived in Rome as normally lived in Jerusalem. No synagogue of the period has yet been identified in Rome (a synagogue in Ostia, the port of ancient Rome, was excavated in 1963). But six Jewish catacombs or underground burial areas have been discovered around Rome, and from inscriptions in these we know the names of eleven Roman synagogues. The ordinary Romans of this period cremated their dead, but Jews (and, in due course, Christians) buried theirs, and so the bodies had to be deposited at a deeper level. The soft tufa limestone of the district around Rome was rather easily tunnelled, and galleries were driven through it lined with recesses in which the dead were placed. None of the Christian catacombs of Rome goes back to New Testament times, but the earliest go back to the second century. One of the earliest is the Cemetery of Priscilla on the Via Salaria, but what connection it has with Paul's friend of that name is uncertain.

The dome of St Peter's, built over the burial ground where the Apostle is traditionally believed to have been buried.

A rock tomb in one of the limestone catacombs. Jews and Christians did not cremate their dead, but buried them on hewn shelves sealed with stone.

Biblical references Revelation 14:8; 17:1-19:3

The book of the Revelation was written against the background of the persecution of Christians by the Roman Empire. Rome is prominent in the book, but not by name. She is referred to as 'Babylon the great', situated on seven hills, 'the great city which has dominion over the kings of the earth'. In language similar to that used by Old Testament prophets to proclaim the downfall of oppressive powers in their days, the impending destruction of 'Babylon the great' is described. But what happened? The empire ultimately capitulated to the church, and Rome became a great Christian metropolis. John's Master taught that the best way to destroy an enemy is to turn him into a friend, and John might have been surprised, but not displeased, could he have foreseen that, 250 years after his day, the persecuting city would embrace the faith which once it tried to exterminate.

There is no place on earth so full of memorials of Christian antiquity as Rome, even if they are nearly all of post-apostolic date.

The Romans mastered the use of the arch and pushed on to pioneer the building of the dome, like the one in their remarkable Pantheon in Rome. Volcanic dust, readily available for use, made a strong kind of concrete.

128

Acknowledgments

Designer: Peter Wyart, Three's Company

Picture Editor: Gill Rennie.

Illustrations: James Macdonald, except pp 29, 44, 59 by Paul Wyart

Photographs (credited by page number)

Gordon Gray: Jesus back cover (main), 1, 6/7 (main) 9 (top), 10, 12 (top inset), 14/5, 16/7 (main), 18, 19, 24, 25, 26/7 main, 30-4, 38, 40/1, 44, 45, 47, 50 (top), 52-5, 57-63 Paul 106-10

F. Nigel Hepper: Paul 69 (bottom)

Paul Marsh: Paul 98

Metropolitan Museum of Art, The Cloisters Collection, Purchase 1950: Paul 79 (right)

Adrian Neilson: Jesus 12/3 (except top inset), 20-2, 23 (bottom), 27 (inset), 28, 35-7, 39, 42, 43, 46, 48/9, 51, 56 Paul 111-5

Gill Rennie: front cover (main), Jesus 5, 7 (inset), 8, 9 (bottom), 11, 16 (inset), 23 (top), 50 (bottom) Paul 65, 86-9, 91, (top), 92-7, 99 (bottom), 100-3, 105, 116-27

Bible Scene Slide Tours/Maurice Thompson. (These photographs are part of a series of slide lectures available from Bible Scene, covering New Testament lands. Paul 69 (top), 70, 73, 79-84, 90, 104

Cliff Townsend: Paul 71, 72, 74-7, 78 (top)

Margaret Wallace: Paul 91 (bottom)

Printed in Italy by

New Interlitho S.p.A. - Milan